THE IMMEDIATE CARE PROCESS

Emotional and Psychological Resilience

SIMON MARYAN

© **The Immediate Care Process**

Copyright: Simon Maryan © 2020

All rights reserved. Except as permitted under current legislation no part of this work may be photocopied, stored in a retrieval system, published, performed in public, adapted or broadcast, transmitted, recorded or reproduced in any form or by any means, without the prior permission in writing of the copyright owners. Enquiries should be addressed to

hello@immediatecareprocess.com

Cover Design: Mishi Bellamy

ISBN: 978-1-716-49306-5

All rights reserved

There is nothing permanent except change. Change is the only constant. Change alone is unchanging."

Heraclitus

We must embrace change, welcome it, and change the frame we place around it and shed a positive light on change. Change is our ally when we perceive it as such, it is how we continue to redefine ourselves as we work towards being who and how we want to be. We must also accept that this never stops, it is a process we are working through to our final day, and this is exciting as it leaves us open to so many opportunities and possibilities to explore ourselves and life.

Simon Maryan

This book is dedicated to everyone suffering with their mental health. Know that every day you get up and do anything is a positive and shows your strength and resilience to win the battle with your mind. These tools are for you because you matter, you are loved, and the world is a better place with you in it.

It is also to honour absent friends who lost their battle with their mind, your absence is felt deeply every day, and it is this loss that inspired the creation of the Immediate Care Process and this book.

You are loved always.

WELCOME

Welcome to the Immediate Care Process. You are taking part in an experience that will open up new avenues of growth, new thought processes and new learnings, as well as providing you with new communication skills and the opportunity for significant and rapid personal change as well as helping others in crisis.

The learnings you will experience have assisted many thousands of people in creating more of what they want in their lives, and less of what they don't want. For many, this training is the first step in a journey of growth and change in their lives resulting in a greater sense of freedom.

The experience of this programme is unique to every individual, so feel free to explore all the possibilities while you are participating. Ask all the questions you have, and seek out all the assistance you would like. If you have any questions or require any assistance or information, we would be delighted to be of service. Contact us at the address below: hello@immediatecareprocess.com

Our commitment is to assist you to achieve your outcomes. So, be clear about what you want. Be focused on your own success, and above all, ENJOY!

Simon Maryan

ACKNOWLEDGEMENTS

I want to acknowledge the many people with whom I have had the fortune of studying and learning with in the fields of Psychology, Psychotherapy, Neuro Linguistics, Hypnosis and Coaching. We are indebted to all of them for their influence on this programme – I apologise for any omission.

Prof David Alexander, Prof Bessel van der Kolk MD, Dan Siegel MD, Allan Score PhD, Steven Porges PhD, Peter Levine PhD, Bill O'Hanlon, Ruth Lanius MD PhD, Pat Ogden PhD, Ruth Buczynski PhD, Christina Hall, Judith Lowe, Judith DeLozier, John Grinder, Perry Zeus, Dr Shayne Tracy, Stephen Brooks,

Richard Bandler, Robert Dilts, Charles Faulkner, Mihaly Csikszentmihalyi, Jeremy Lazarus, Dr Lisa de Dijk

I am also grateful to my students and clients who continue to remind me how much I don't know and help motivate me to continue learning.

ABOUT THE AUTHORS

SIMON MARYAN

Born in England, the son of a Royal Marine Pilot, he grew up in the Far East, Middle East and Africa and studied at boarding school in Somerset.

He joined the Royal Marines as a boy soldier and his career led him to becoming a very adept operating across the globe in hostile and extremely stressful environments. Now an international speaker, author, trainer and coach, Simon utilises lessons from a life of action along with many years spent training in psychology, psychotherapy and coaching to help people prepare for and overcome trauma and other stressful situations.

Simon survived three separate kidnappings which developed and then formed an extremely strong psychological and mental resilience which he now shares with people through his well-attended speaking engagements and training courses. He delivers a compilation of keynote, motivational and inspirational talks for a wide variety of clients, internationally. Some of these have included the UK Military, FBI, New York Police Department, NYPD Hostage Negotiation Team, oil and gas, and other energy companies, global banks and various UK Government departments in need of his expertise.

Since 2010 he has also provided voluntary charitable services in mental health for the serving UK Military, Veterans and all Uniformed Services. He does this through tacharity he cofounded with his friend and co-therapist, David Bellamy.

Simon has been frequently featured on BBC, STV, BFBS, BBC Radio, Northsound Radio, Forces News, Sunday Mirror, Financial Times and various International podcasts and interviews.

www.simonmaryan.com

TABLE OF CONTENTS

welcome iv

Acknowledgements v

About The Authors vi

PART 1 FOUNDATION TRAINING

What Is The Immediate Care Process? 2

Your Outcomes For This Training 4

The Principles For Success 5

Outcomes & Their Effect 7

Conditions For Using These Skills 9

Cause & Effect 11

The Mind-Body Connection 16

Neurological Connections 18

A Communication Model 20

Filters 22

Sensory Acuity 28

Observing Other People 30

Sensory Acuity Exercises 32

Rapport 34

Definitions 35

Process 36

Indicators Of Rapport 37

Pacing And Leading	38
How To Create Rapport	40
Representational Systems And Language	43
V: Visual Representation System	45
A: Auditory Representational System	47
K: Kinaesthetic Representational System	49
Ad: Auditory Digital Representational System	51
Representational System Preference	52
Scoring The Questionnaire	56
Predicates	58
Predicate Words	59
List Of Predicate Phrases	61
Examples Of Predicate Phrases At Work	63
Eye Accessing Cues Eye Pattern Chart	65
Elicitation Of Eye Patterns	67
Some Tips For Eliciting Eye Patterns	70
Eye Tracking Exercises	71
Summary Of Eye Accessing Cues	73
Overlapping Representational Systems	75
Synesthesia	77
Auditory-Tactile Synesthesia	78
Misophonia	79
Mirror-Touch Synesthesia	80
Lexical-Gustatory Synesthesia	81

Other Forms 82

Modalities & Submodalities 83

    Visual Submodalities 84
    Auditory Submodalities 84
    Kinaesthetic Submodalities 84
    Critical And Driver Submodalities 85
    Analogue And Digital Submodalities 85
    Associated And Dissociated 85

Possible Uses Of Submodalities 87

Eliciting Submodalities 89

Using Submodalities 90

Submodality Exercises 93

Tips For Successful Submodality Interventions 95

Memory & The Limbic System 97

Submodality Tracking Worksheet Limbic System Overview
Perceptual Blindness & Conscious Overload 99

Brain Activity And Brainwaves 101

What Are Brainwaves? 102

The 5 Main Types Of Brainwaves 104

    Gamma Brainwaves 105
    Beta Brainwaves 106
    Alpha Brainwaves 107
    Theta Brainwaves 107
    Delta Brainwaves 108

Influences On Your State Of Mind 110

Emotional Response Vs Decisions 112

Beliefs 118

Identifying Limiting Beliefs 121

The Extended Logical Levels Of Change 123

    Introduction 123
    Environment 124
    Opportunity 124
    Constraints 125
    Behaviour 126
    Action 126
    Reaction 127
    Capability 127
    Intellect 128
    Emotion 128
    Beliefs And Values 129
    Motivation 130
    Permission 130
    Identity 131
    Role 132
    Purpose 133
    Vision 133
    Ambition 134
    Personal Exploration Exercise 134

The Behavioural Change Learning Cycle 136

    Four Stages Of Learning 138
    Behavioural Change Learning Cycle 138

The Intentional Change Model 140

Anchoring 148

Uses Of Anchoring 150

    Present State + Resources = Desired State 150

Five Keys To Anchoring 152

The Anchoring Process 153

The Anchoring Process Visual Guide 156

PART 2: PSYCHOLOGICAL SKILLS

Negative Thought Pattern Interrupt 158

The Process 160

The Detail 162

Whole Brain State And Anchor 165

The Process 169

    Part 1: Whole Brain State 169
    Part 2: Anchor 170
    Eye Patterning And Reimprinting 171

What Are Imprints & How Are They Created 173

Modelling Others Perspectives 177

Identifying And Working With Imprints 178

Brick Walls & Feeling Stuck 179

Eye Patterning And Reimprinting Process 182

Swish Patterns 187

    Keys To Successful Swish Patterns 192

Swish Pattern Script 194

Designer Swish 196

Final Note 197

Recommended Reading 198

PART 1
FOUNDATION TRAINING

WHAT IS THE IMMEDIATE CARE PROCESS?

Immediate Care Process is an amalgamation of several fields of Psychology (sport, cognitive, behavioural, positive), Hypnosis, Neuroscience, Psychotherapy and Neuro Linguistics. This incredibly powerful blend of several schools of thought creates a deep and broad view of how our minds work, how we decide on what's important for us, what's a threat, what's stressful and what we decide to do with that information.

The Immediate Care Process takes advantage of NLP's modelling process, often called a **Psychology of Excellence**, is discovering and taking on the beliefs, values, behaviours and mental sequencing found in people who are outstanding in their field and utilising these in yourself and others. It is also finding examples of when you have been excellent, finding out how you were doing that and replicating it in different areas of your life.

This course is all about Emotional & Psychological Resilience and provides you with easy to learn, simple to use, powerful psychological tools that you can use with yourself or anyone else experiencing a mental health crisis. The course begins with a foundation in how we process information, how we communicate this and how it can go wrong when we become overloaded and overwhelmed.

After the underpinning theory, the next step is to learn the skills themselves through a series of explanations, demonstrations and then you practice them yourself with a partner or group of three, then we debrief after each exercise.

Learning this way means you get plenty of practical hands on experience from three different perspectives, 1) as the client, 2) as the practitioner and 3) as an observer giving feedback to the practitioner, as well as the feedback from the client

YOUR OUTCOMES FOR THIS TRAINING

Before you begin, I would like you to take a few moments to think about why you bought this book or attended the course, what was the purpose of it?

Now write your desired outcomes for working through this book and learning how to use the tools it provides, what do you want to achieve by learning these tools? Make your outcomes so significant that this will be the most important and the most impactful programme you have ever worked through.

So get yourself a notepad or type into a document on your computer or tablet and at the end of the programme you can look at what you wrote and identify what was met, what wasn't, what do you still need, what exceeded your expectations?

Answering these questions will help you to keep learning and ensure that you maintain your direction and achieve your purpose.

THE PRINCIPLES FOR SUCCESS

The following model is useful in a wide variety of contexts, in fact, it is difficult to imagine a situation where it would not be useful to use this model to enhance your chances of success

1. **Know What You Want To Achieve.** If you can define what you want then it will be more achievable. Don't start anything without knowing what you want in advance.

2. **Use Your Observation Skills.** See and sense what is going on in your life as you proceed to your goal. What new things are you noticing in yourself? What new things are you noticing in others? Seek and take feedback.

3. **Have Behavioural Flexibility.** Be willing to do whatever it takes (remembering to be ecological) to achieve success. With enough rapport and enough behavioural flexibility, you can greatly increase your chances of achieving your goals.

4. **Build and Maintain Rapport.** Create a climate of trust and co-operation.

5. **Operate From a Physiology and Psychology of Excellence.** Operate from a totally resourceful state. Do things that will empower you and others.

6. **Take Action.** Without action there are no results and change will not occur.

OUTCOMES & THEIR EFFECT

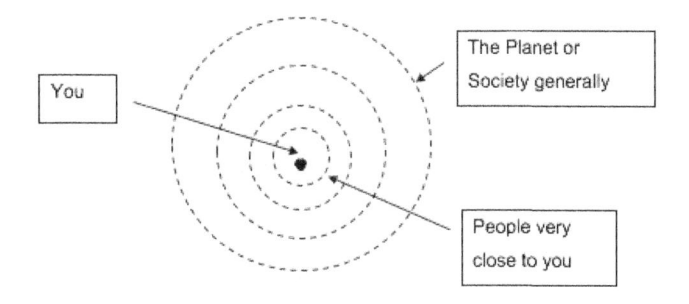

As someone who helps others through the use of the skills taught in this book, we work with others to help them realise what changes they want and need to make and how to make those changes in a way that has the most positive impact on them and their life. When we focus on the outcome of reaching specific goals, we help people take a step back and have a global view, where they can appreciate the impact the outcome/s will have on them, their family, friends, colleagues etc. With this information they can make a much more informed choice as to how best to achieve an ecological and congruent outcome.

Working towards and achieving any goal creates a wave and delivers an outcome or set of outcomes and this process affects others around you through the ripple effect. It is extremely important to be aware of the effect decisions and actions have on those around you and this poses several questions:

- What compromises, sacrifices are acceptable?
- What do they need to stop doing?
- What do they need to start doing?
- What do they need to do differently?

CONDITIONS FOR USING THESE SKILLS

There are several ways to facilitate the right conditions for working with people in an successful way, a way that is appropriate for you and anyone you help using these principles.

Here are some of the ways to do this:

- Asking the pre-intervention questions below
- Testing your interventions
- Considering the situation from different viewpoints by Shifting Perspectives
- Considering the Logical Levels of Change
- Taking into account the Neuro Linguistic Pre-suppositions (handout) – does the intervention conflict with any of them?
- How does the intervention fit with your own personal philosophy?
- Using your observational skills to notice body language signals suggesting that either yourself or

the person you are working with is not 100% certain about making the changes

Pre-Intervention Questions

In addition, there are some useful questions to ask before doing any intervention:

1. What's going on, what's happening now? (Score 0-10)
2. What do you want/need to change or be different? (Score 010)
3. How will you know if things have changed in the way you want them to?
4. What's going to happen if you do, if you don't?:
    - negative (if any)? (if so, address them before doing attempting to make any changes)
    - positive?
    - Is there anything else?
5. On a scale of 0-100, how OK is it for you to do this / make this change now?

NB. If it is not 100%, find out what is missing. Interventions work best when we are 100% willing to do it. It is strongly recommended never to proceed unless the person is 100% willing.

CAUSE & EFFECT

Cause and Effect is all about re-directing your focus more on the "How" rather than the "why". It has a very practical application with the aim of training you to be in charge of your own mind, the way you think, your views towards past and present events, and mostly your approach towards life.

Cause and Effect is a language or communication pattern, between one element and the other, it occurs mostly within oneself. Cause and effect are that something definitely leads to another or makes something else happen.

Statistics has it that a huge number of people focus more on effects and very few people focus on the causes, this is the polar opposite of what is most effective and useful, especially when you understand how this works in real time.

Take for instance, "I can't concentrate on this project, because I'm having a hard time with life", the "because" in that statement has led to the effect. Effect focuses more on blame, you blame the other for what you can't achieve. The aim of this training is to shift your focus on to the causes and how to achieve it without putting effects in the way.

"I couldn't finish up the job, because I wasn't in the right frame of mind, I got pissed off by someone ", these are just excuses.

Instead get focused on what's important and useful, be determined to achieve something each day, concentrate more on the causes and the effects will take place less and less.

Alternatively, "I got the job done despite the challenges I had at work today," I'm a doctor today despite studying for 15 years, I didn't give up even after I failed and was withheld for some years". This is the absolute determination; you don't have to blame someone else for what you failed to achieve.

When you look back in the future, it wouldn't be nice saying things like "I would have been this, if it wasn't for that," come on. The era of such excuses is gone, be the driver of your life, decide which route to take and the amount of fuel you need for your tank.

We are all capable of getting what we focus on and put our minds to most of the time, when you get fixed on solutions and not your limitations. The "Milton Model" Milton Erickson MD, enlightens us more about cause and effect, with experiments on his patients in their unconscious mind, this language pattern tends to put you in a trance.

In Neuro-Linguistic Programming (NLP), Cause and Effect are said to be in line with rules and beliefs. They are simply statements that show our belief in how things work; it's either A causes B, or by doing A it makes B happen. It's pertinent to note that, believing something doesn't make it true.

A distortion people often make is assumptions, like someone, can put you in a certain state or make you feel a certain way, feeling this way is quite common and debilitating. The"If-Then" statement is also a common one in cause and effect, "if I work hard, then I can take care of my family," remember one thing leads to another.

CAUSE & EFFECT

COMPARING THE IMPACT OF THESE 2 TYPES OF INFLUENCE ON OUR LIVES

SIMON MARYAN

CAUSE = HOW	EFFECT = WHAT
I influence and take responsibility for everything that happens in my life.	My life is random, I can't affect or control what I think, say or do or anyone else.
I control where I work, what I do and how. The choice is mine.	I have no choice in where I work, what I do or how. I have to do what others want me to do.
I am responsible for maintaining the relationships in my life and who I have relationships with.	I have no choice or control of the relationships in my life or who I have relationships with.
I accept that I have had control over how I have responded to everything that has happened to me and that I have had influence over my life.	I have had no control over how I have responded to everything that has happened to me and I have had no influence over my life.

Often, the statements open up to solutions, with the model questioning technique. It opens up the unconscious mind. A statement could go this way "I make her angry," the model question comes in How exactly do you make her angry?" This is a good way of getting rid of the effects. The graphic below explores this:

THE MIND-BODY CONNECTION

The field of psychoneuroimmunology has witnessed an explosion of empirical findings during the last two decades. Research has documented the mechanisms through which stressful emotions alter white blood cell function. Stress diminishes white blood cell response to viral infected cells and to cancer cells. Moreover, vaccination is less effective in those who are stressed and wounds heal less readily in those who are stressed. While stress decreases the activity of some white blood cells, stress does not compromise the function of all types of white blood cells. Indeed, some types of autoimmune disease, which involve particular subsets of white blood cells, are exacerbated by stress. The literature documents the efficacy of talk-therapy interventions in altering immune system parameters and enhancing the body's ability to combat disease. The literature also documents the impact of the chronic stress of poverty on immune system function.

Littrell J. The mind-body connection: not just a theory anymore. Soc Work Health Care. 2008;46(4):17-37. doi: 10.1300/j010v46n04_02. PMID: 18589562.

The Mind and Body are the Same System

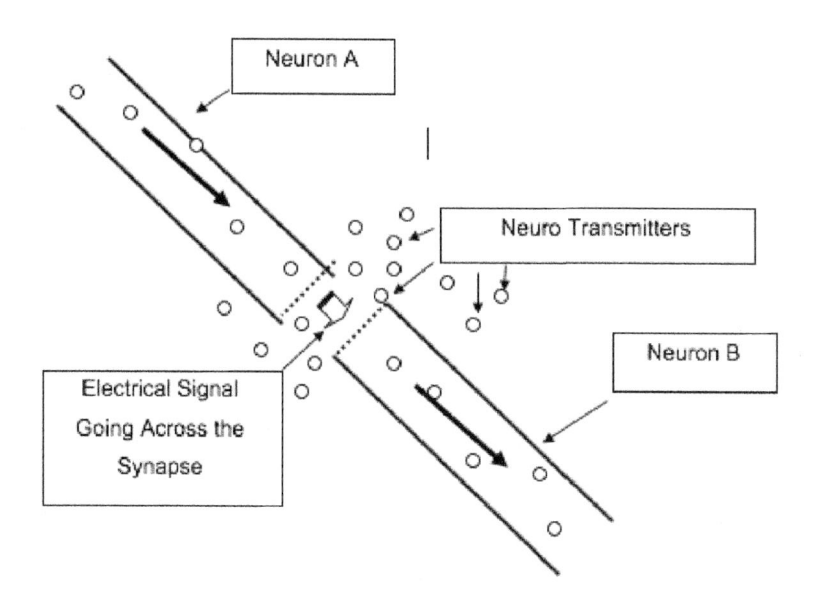

[Diagram showing Neuron A sending an Electrical Signal Going Across the Synapse via Neuro Transmitters to Neuron B]

"Every Cell is Eavesdropping on Your Internal Dialogue" - Deepak Chopra

What does this actually mean in terms of our health, growth and development, happiness?

NEUROLOGICAL CONNECTIONS

There are: $(10\ 10)11$

Neurological connections in your body. That's the number 1 with 10 zeros after it, written eleven times!

100,000,000,000,000,000,000,
000,000,000,000,000,000,000,000,000,
000,000,000,000,000,000,000,000,000,000,
000,000,000,000,000,000,000,000,000,000,000!

So thinking about Deepak Chopra's quote in conjunction with the staggering number of neurological connections, that means that everything you say to yourself and what others say to you is picked up by your mind and body. Now depending on the effect this dialogue has on you, positive or negative, determines the influence it has on your cells and your genes, because the end caps of your genes (Telomeres) have switches that can be turned on or off and thus altering you at the genetic level. Environmental factors have a phenomenal influence on this process.

Reflect on how you have been physically, mentally and emotionally affected in times of high stress. How did you think, feel, talk and behave differently in comparison to the times when everything was flowing smoothly in your life?

Take a moment to write down the differences.

A COMMUNICATION MODEL

Originally conceived and developed by *John Grinder* and NLP or Neuro Linguistic Programming began as a model of how we communicate and interact with ourselves and others. The NLP communication model explains how we process the information that comes in from outside us and what we do with it inside.

In **NLP** terms, the belief is that *"The map is not the territory,"* so the internal representations that we make about an outside event are not essentially the event itself. What happens is that there is an external event and we run that event through our internal processing. We make an Internal Representation (I/R) of that event. The I/R of the event then combines with a physiology to create a state. The word "State" refers to the internal emotional state of the individual, " happy, sad, motivated etc.

Did you ever notice that people treat their perceptions differently? Some people have to "see" certain relationships between things, where others have to have it explained so they can "hear it". Still others have to "get a grasp or a feeling" for the relationships. This is the essence of this Communication Model.

So, the external event comes in through the sensory input channels and is filtered and managed by our neurology. As we manage the perception of the event, we delete, distort, and generalise the information according to the following processes that filter our perception.

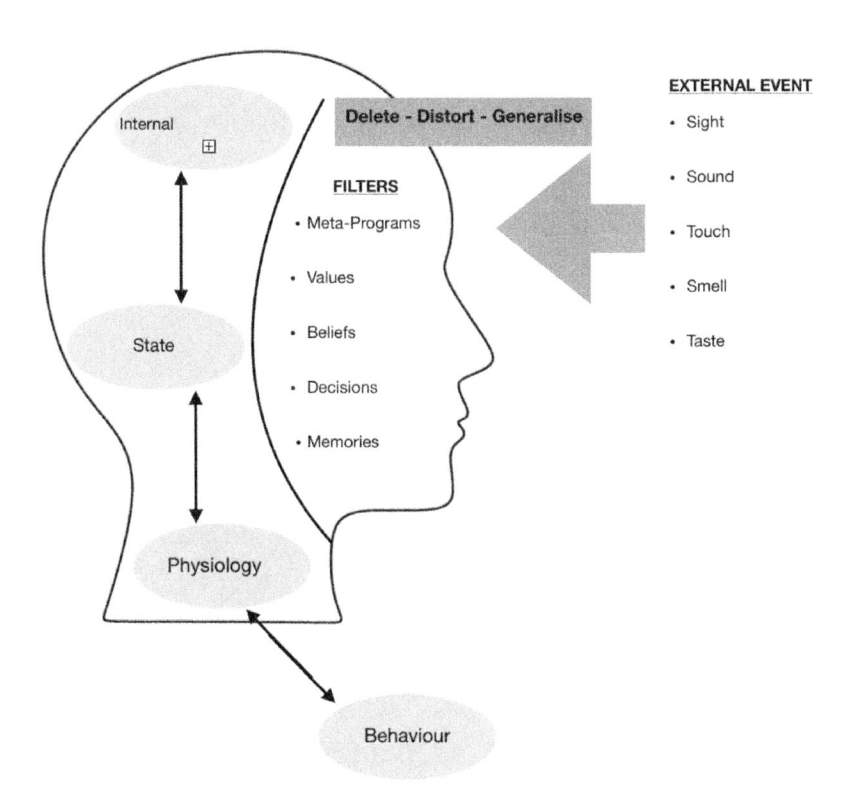

EXTERNAL EVENT
- Sight
- Sound
- Touch
- Smell
- Taste

Delete - Distort - Generalise

FILTERS
- Meta-Programs
- Values
- Beliefs
- Decisions
- Memories

Internal

State

Physiology

Behaviour

FILTERS

Deletion:

Deletion occurs when we selectively pay attention to certain aspects of our experience and not others. We overlook or omit others. Without deletion, we would be faced with too much information. Maybe you already are overloaded with information and you feel like you have too much.

Distortion:

Distortion occurs when we misrepresent reality by making shifts in our experience of sensory data. In Indian philosophy, there is a well-known story of distortion in the rope versus snake analogy.

A man walking along the road sees what he believes to be a snake and yells SNAKE." However, upon arriving at that place he is relieved as he discovers that what he sees only a piece of rope.

Distortion is an important component to the NLP Communication Model and can be used to motivate ourselves. Motivation can happen when we actually misrepresent, change or garble the material that has come into our neurology. The information has been changed by one of our filtering systems.

I hate all Indian music because I have heard Ravi Shankar and did not like it."

Usually, the conscious mind can only handle seven (plus or minus 2) pieces of information at any given time. It gets overloaded. So, we tend to oversimplify, make decisions and set attitudes based on insufficient information. It's critical to understand this in terms of the larger NLP Communication Model. Generalisation is very common in the world today. Everybody does it. It's is a result of the digital information causing information overload and taking over sensibility.

Of course, we all know many people can't even handle this number, and I know you know people who can only process "1 (plus or minus 2)." How about you?

Try this: Can you name more than 7 products in a given product category, say cigarettes? Most people will be able to name 2, maybe 3 products in a category of low interest and usually no more than 9 in a category of high interest. There is a reason for this.

If we did not actively delete information all the time, we would end up with much too much information coming in. In fact, you may have even heard that psychologists say that if we were simultaneously aware of all of the sensory information that was coming in, we would go crazy. That is why we filter the information.

At its best, generalisation is one of the ways that we learn - taking the information we have and drawing broad conclusions about the meaning of those conclusions. So, the question is, when two people have the same stimulus, why do they not have the same response? The answer is, because we delete, distort, and generalise the information from the outside that comes in from our senses based on one of five filters. The filters of the NLP Communication Model are **Meta Programs, Belief Systems, Values, Decisions, and Memories**.

Meta-Programs:

The first of these NLP filters is Meta Programs. Knowing someone's Meta Programs can help you clearly and closely predict people's states, and therefore predict their actions and behaviours. Meta Programs are clearly outlined in Tad James book Time-Line Therapy, and the Basis of Personality One important point about Meta Programs: they are not good or bad, they are just the way someone handles information.

Values:

The next filter in NLP is Values. Values are essentially an evaluation filter. They are how we decide whether our actions are good or bad, right or wrong and how we feel about our actions. Values are arranged in a hierarchy

The Immediate Care Process

with the most important one typically being at the top and lesser ones below that. They are also discussed in Tad James book Time-Line Therapy, and the Basis of Personality. Each of us has a different NLP Communication model of the world (an internal model about how the world is), and our Values are the result of our model of the world. When we communicate with ourselves or someone else, if our model of the world conflicts with our values or someone else's values, then there is going to be a conflict. Richard Bandler says, t live up to."

Values are what people typically move toward or away from (see Meta Programs). They are our attractions or repulsions in life. They are basically a deep, unconscious belief system about what's important, and Values can change with context too. That is, you probably have certain values about what you want in a relationship and what you want in a business. Your values about what you want in one and in the other may be different. And actually, if they're not, it's possible that you may have trouble with both. Since values are context related, they may also be state related.

s important to discover what beliefs they have that cause them to do what they do. We also want to find out the disabling beliefs, the ones that do not allow them to do what they want to do.

25

Memories:

The fourth filter is our memories. In fact, a number of psychologists say that the present plays a very small part in our behaviour. They believe that as we get older, our reactions in the present are more and more just reactions to gestalts (collections of memories that are organised in a certain way) of past memories, We can use Time-Line Therapy® to make changes in our memories for a positive result.

Decisions:

The fifth filter is the decisions that we have made in the past.

Decisions may create new beliefs or may just affect our perceptions through time. The problem with many decisions is that they were made either unconsciously or at a very early age and are forgotten. But the effect is still there. We can also make changes to the limiting decisions in our past using Time-Line Therapy® techniques.

These five filters will determine how we internally represent an event that is occurring now. It is our internal representation that puts us in a certain state and creates a certain physiology. The state in which we find ourselves, will determine our behaviour, and the NLP Communication Model will determine how we process all the information from the outside world.

Now think of time and situation where you can recognise these filters at play in a negative way and then a positive way. How did they influence your communication model and how were the outcomes different?

SENSORY ACUITY

Sensory Acuity is the ability to gain awareness of how other people automatically (often non-verbally) respond. Although we are rarely trained to perceive another person's automatic (and in some cases, unconscious) responses, almost everyone is able to do it quite easily with people who they know. We can normally tell if a close friend or family member has had a bad day, just by a simple glance at them or listening to the way they say 'Hello'. By observing people who we don't know quite so well through our visual, auditory and kinaesthetic senses, we can notice responses that indicate a tremendous amount of new information and help us accelerate the process we do naturally with people we know well.

Why is this useful?

- To enable you to communicate even more effectively.
- To determine the client's response to a process that affects and changes behaviour. Once you

know your outcome, you can determine through your senses whether you are on track or off track with your client. Once you are more sensory aware, you are able to notice when something is not working and you are able to change your direction and reach your outcome.

- Sensory acuity is one of the principles of success.
- Having excellent sensory acuity will enable you to notice whether the client's conscious and unconscious messages are congruent.
- Using sensory-based information can often prevent us 'mind-reading' or jumping to conclusions about someone.

Example:

- You see someone you don't know well, and you notice their arms are folded, what does that mean?
- You see someone who's face is flushed, what does that mean?
- You hear someone's voice change to be higher pitched, shrill and louder. What does that mean?
- You feel the atmosphere in a room change. What does that mean?

OBSERVING OTHER PEOPLE

Below are some common signs to become aware of, that indicate what someone is currently experiencing, feeling.

1.   B Breathing Rate

Fast - Slow

Location

High - — - - - - - Low

2.   L Lower Lip Size

Lines - — - - - - - - No Lines

3.   E Eyes Focus

Focused - Defocused

Pupil Dilation

Constricted -
Dilated

4.   S Skin Tonus (The Tone of the Muscles)

Shiny - Not
Shiny

5.   S Skin Colour Change

Light - — - - - - - - - - - -
Dark

Other points – tilt of head, eye brow movements, lip/mouth movements, angle of spine, clusters of gestures.

SENSORY ACUITY EXERCISES

Find someone you can work with for these exercises

Exercise 1 (pairs)

1. Client thinks of someone they like. The Practitioner calibrate.
2. Client then 'clears their screen' and thinks of someone they don't like. The Practitioner calibrate.
3. Client thinks of one of those 2 people, without saying which one, and the Practitioner has to guess which one the client is thinking of.
4. Repeat until the Practitioners have got it right 3 times and switch round.

Exercise 2

1. Client adopts a posture.
2. The Practitioner takes a mental image of the client and then closes his/her eyes.
3. Client makes a minor relatively shift in posture (make it relatively obvious)

The Immediate Care Process

4. The Practitioner opens eyes, and notices the change
5. Repeat a few times, making the shifts in posture progressively smaller and less obvious.

Exercise 3

Similar to Exercise 2 above, except that the Practitioner adopts the exact posture of the client in step 2. Then, in step 4, the Practitioner notices the change by adopting the same posture as the client now has.

Exercise 4 – Auditory Acuity

1. The Practitioner has his/her back to the client.
2. Client thinks of someone they like and counts out loud from 1 to 10. The Practitioner calibrate.
3. Client thinks of someone they dislike and counts out loud from 1 to 10. The Practitioner calibrate.
4. Client thinks of one person and counts to 10 out loud. The Practitioner guesses which one.
5. Repeat, with client counting out loud from 1 to 5.

Exercise 5

1. The Practitioner has his/her back to the client.
2. Client thinks of something they really want to do and says 'Yes'. The Practitioner calibrate.
3. Client thinks of something they really don't want to do and says 'Yes'. The Practitioner calibrate.

33

4. Client thinks of one of the two things and says 'Yes'. The Practitioner guess which one.

RAPPORT

Rapport is the ability to relate to others in a way that creates a climate of trust and understanding. the purpose of rapport is to establish a feeling of comfort and commonality between people, in order to be better able to influence them in a positive way.

Being in Rapport also helps people to see each other's point of view, to be on each other's same wavelength, and to appreciate each other's feelings. The aim is to be able to establish rapport with any person(s), at any moment in time. When people are like each other, they like each other. Rapport is a process of creating trust, not necessarily "liking" people.

DEFINITIONS

Matching:

Replicating exactly some aspect of a person's physiology. e.g: your right hand against your chin, my right hand against my chin

Mirroring:

Replicating the mirror image of an aspect of someone's physiology. This results in even deeper rapport even quicker. e.g: When facing each other, your right hand against your chin, my left hand against my chin.

Cross Matching/Mirroring:

Matching/mirroring one aspect of a person's physiology with a different aspect of your own physiology, such as their breathing with your finger movement.

PROCESS

Rapport is the process of responsiveness, at the unconscious level, established by matching and mirroring. This is replicating or reflecting aspects of the client's non-verbal behaviour back to them. This enables the unconscious mind to accept and begin processing suggestions.

NB:

- Avoid too much rapport if the client is in a negative state, or use cross-over mirroring
- Make sure you have a positive intention for the other person(s), otherwise it will probably feel like manipulation.
- Use your common sense

INDICATORS OF RAPPORT

1. Feeling - Practitioner gets feeling of rapport.
2. Colour Change - Client has colour shift.
3. Says Something - Client says something like, "Have we met before?"
4. Leading - Practitioner can begin **Leading** the client.

PACING AND LEADING

(See Bandler, Richard; Grinder, John. *Frogs Into Princes*, page 80)

When the quality of rapport is good it is possible to encourage an individual to follow the movements, and potentially the thinking, which you are using. **Pacing** and **Leading** involves matching someone for a while (pacing) until you have gained a level of rapport sufficient that when you slowly start to change what you are doing; the individual will follow you (leading). In this way you can lead your partner into different (more comfortable) body postures, and also to be able to bring them more into line with your thinking.

Pacing and leading depends on the quality or level of rapport that you build up. If your partner follows your lead unconsciously you have a good level of rapport. If the partner does not follow your lead go back to matching again, observing more attentively (pacing) before leading again. As a rule of thumb:

PACE……… PACE……. PACE…………LEAD

The applications of this technique are many and varied. This can be used when people are upset, angry or defensive, or when you want to change someone's opinion at a meeting. Building rapport puts you in a position to influence them towards win-win situations.

HOW TO CREATE RAPPORT

There are many ways of creating rapport. In three of the most effective to create rapport you:

1. Match non-verbal communication especially voice patterns and eye contact patterns
2. Develop a genuine interest in the other person and in their model of the world 3. Use the 4 R's Principle.

1. Matching non-verbal communication

Create non-verbal rapport using the sound of your voice and your eye contact pattern.

This is the quickest and most useful way to begin. And it's simple - you just aim to approximate the sound of their voice and the way in which they create eye contact.

In general, aim to do as little as is necessary to achieve rapport. You are aiming to be subtle and to create rapport without this process intruding into the person's conscious awareness.

: we strongly recommend that you never, ever, ever match body language such as the person's posture, gestures, movements, etc. Why? Because this mechanical method is too obvious and, in most cases, will quickly be recognised as a manipulative process and, rightly, backfire!

2. Develop a genuine interest in them

This is one of the most effective ways of creating rapport. Here rapport occurs because of your genuine interest in their model of the world i.e., in how they experience life.

3. Use the 4 R's Principle

The 4 R's Principle is an attitude rather than a technique. It involves aiming to ensure that, in their relationship with us, the other person experiences a sense of:

- : They feel that they are respected as unique and equal-with-us individuals
- **Recognition**: Their experience is that we are recognising their verbal and their non-verbal communication and appropriately responding to each of these channels
- **Reassurance**: Their relationship, and their interaction, with us is experienced as nonthreatening especially at the level of Self Esteem

- **Responsibility**: Their experience of communicating with us is effortless and seamless – because we are acting "responsibly" in that we are varying our means of communicating with them to make it easier for them, should they want to do so, to relate with us.

What's the best way to create rapport?

Begin with Method 1 in the early stages of developing your conscious rapport building skills. As your level of skill increases in using some of the more subtle NLP processes such as recognising and responding to body language, using Soft Eyes, using calibration skills, etc. aim to use Methods 2 and 3 alongside one another.

REPRESENTATIONAL SYSTEMS AND LANGUAGE

There is a **Representational System** for each of our senses; this is the way we experience our world. What we actually perceive are representations of what each sensory organ transmits to us.

These representational systems are

Ve Visual External. What you see outside you.

Vi Visual Internal. What you see inside

– visualisation/imagination

Auditory (A)

Ae Auditory External - hearing external sounds

Ai Auditory Internal – recalling/creating internal sounds

Kinaesthetic (K)

Ke External - Tactile Sensations of Touch, Temperature, Moisture

Ki Internal - Remembered Sensations, Emotions, Feelings of Balance & Bodily

Awareness, Proprioceptive Senses

Olfactory (O)

Oe External - Real Time Sensation of Smell

Oi Internal - Remembered sensations of smell linked to specific memories

(G)

Ge External - Real Time

Sensation of Taste

Gi Internal - Remembered sensations of taste linked to specific memories

V: VISUAL REPRESENTATION SYSTEM

The process of translating communication into pictures.

People whose preferred representational system is tend to do some of the following:

- Stand or sit with their heads and/or bodies erects, with their eyes up.

- Breathe from the top of their lungs and their upper shoulders and breathe fairly rapidly.

- Often sit forward in their chair and tend to be organised, neat, well groomed and orderly.

- Appearance is important to them.

- Memorise by seeing pictures, and are less distracted by noise.

- Often have trouble remembering verbal instructions because their minds tend to wander.

- Talk quickly. "A picture is worth a thousands words".

- Use picture descriptions during conversation.

- Interested in how things or your product/service look.

- Want to see things to understand them.

- Like visually based feedback.

- Use gestures that may be high & quick.

A: AUDITORY REPRESENTATIONAL SYSTEM

The process of translating communication into sounds.

People whose preferred representational system is **auditory** tend to do some of the following:

- Move their eyes sideways/from side to side.
- Breathe from the middle of their chest.
- Typically talk to themselves and some even move their lips when they talk to themselves.
- Are easily distracted by noise.
- Can repeat things back to you easily.
- Learn by listening.
- Usually like music and talking on the phone.
- Memorise by steps, procedures, and sequences (sequentially).

- Likes to be TOLD how they're doing.

- Responds to a certain tone of voice or set of words.

- Will be interested in what you have to say about your product/service.

- Medium to fast talkers.

- Translate conversation to sounds associated with topic.

- Excellent at repeating back instructions.

K: KINAESTHETIC REPRESENTATIONAL SYSTEM

The process of checking communication with our feelings.

People whose preferred representational system is **kinaesthetic** tend to do some of the following:

- Breathe from the bottom of their lungs, so you'll see their stomach go in and out when they breathe.

- Often move and talk very slowly.

- Respond to physical rewards and touching.

- Stand closer to people than a visual person does.

- Memorise by doing or walking through something.

- Will be interested in your product/service if it "feels right".

- Check out their feelings prior to expressing their thoughts.

- Are very physical people and like to touch during conversation.

- Like to walk through something before doing it.

- Use gestures that are low and smooth.

AD: AUDITORY DIGITAL REPRESENTATIONAL SYSTEM

The process of internally checking communication by talking to ourselves.

People whose preferred representational system is **auditory digital** tend to do some of the following:

- Spend a fair amount of time talking to themselves.
- Want to know if your product/service "makes sense".
- Can exhibit characteristics of the other major representational systems.
- Speaks in a clipped, crisp monotone.
- Have breathing patterns like an auditory, higher up in the chest.
- Are dissociated from feelings.
- In some professions (eg accounting, law, banking), Ad is almost 'de rigeur'.

REPRESENTATIONAL SYSTEM PREFERENCE

For each of the following statements, please place a number next to every phrase.

Use the following system to indicate your preferences:

4 = Most accurately describes your preference

3 = Next best description of your preference

2 = Next best after 3 above of your preference

1 = Least likely description of your preference

At this point, ignore the reference to a, b, c and d.

1. Generally I make important decisions based on:

    a. ___ which way looks best to me

    b. ___ which way sounds the best to me

    c. ___ review, analysis and consideration of the issues

    d. ___ my gut level feelings, what feels best to me

2. **During a heated debate, I am most likely to be influenced by:**

   a. __ people's tone of voice

   b. __ whether or not I can see the other person's point of view

   c. __ the logic of the other person's argument

   d. __ how I feel about the topics

3. **During a meeting, I like information to be presented:**

   a. __ in a way that is neat and tidy, with pictures and diagrams

   b. __ in a way that I can grasp and that I can get a hands-on experience

   c. __ in a logical, rational way, so that I can understand

   d. __ in the form of a conversation, so that we can discuss and I can ask questions

4. **My favourite hobbies and pastimes typically involve:**

   a. __ listening to music, the radio or talking with people

   b. __ watching films and other visual arts

The Immediate Care Process

   c. ___ doing sport, activities and generally moving about
   d. ___ reading, learning, analysing and generally using my mind

5. I tend to resolve problems by:

   a. ___ looking at the situation and all the alternatives, possibly using diagrams
   b. ___ talking through the situation with friends or colleagues
   c. ___ analysing the situation and choosing the approach that makes most sense
   d. ___ trusting my intuition and gut feelings

6. When with my friends:

   a. a ___ I enjoy watching how they interact and behave
   b. d ___ I tend to hug them, or sit close to them, when speaking to them
   c. c ___ I am interested in their rationale, reasons and ideas when talking to them
   d. b ___ I enjoy talking and listening to them

7. I prefer to learn a particular aspect of a sport or activity by:

55

a. a ___ Watching how the teacher or coach does it

b. d ___ Having the teacher or coach adjust my body into the right position

c. b ___ Listening to explanations, discussing and asking questions

d. c ___ Understanding the reasons and rationale for doing it in a certain way

8. When at a presentation, I am most interested by

a. c ___ The logic and rational of the presentation

b. b ___ The tone of voice and way the presenter speaks

c. a ___ The visual aids used by the presenter

d. d ___ The opportunity to get to grips with the content, perhaps by actually doing an activity

SCORING THE QUESTIONNAIRE

STEP TWO: Transfer the scores above into the following table.

For example, if your scores for question 8 are:

- '1' for the first statement,
- '4' for the second statement,
- '3' for the third statement and
- '2' for the fourth statement,

then in row 8 you would put '1' in column 'c', '4' in column 'b', '3' in column 'a' and '2' in column 'd'.

	a	b	c	d
1				
2				
3				

4				
5				
6				
7				
8				
TOTAL	**V =**	**A =**	**Ad =**	**K =**

STEP THREE:

The totals give an indication of your relative preference for each of the four major representational systems (a = Visual, b = Auditory, c = Auditory Digital, d = Kinaesthetic). Remember, these scores are preferences, **not** statements about capability or about who you are as a person.

PREDICATES

When listening to a person talk, you will often hear people use **'Predicates'.** These are words and phrases (primarily verbs, adverbs and adjectives) that often presuppose one of the representational systems. As you listen to a person talk over a period of time, you may discover that a majority of the predicates that are used refer to one representational system more often than any of the others. This is a clue to what type of sensory experience this person is most likely to notice.

This most frequent use of one system over the others is called a person's **Primary Representational System**. Its use can be thought of as habitual, and it often becomes more evident during stressful situations for the individual. This system is usually the one a person makes the most distinctions in and can be recognised by **Physiology and Predicates.**

Overlapping Representational Systems is the process of taking a person from their most used or preferred representational system to the least preferred.

Simon Maryan

PREDICATE WORDS

The Immediate Care Process

VISUAL	AUDITORY	KINAESTHETIC	AUDIT DIGIT
See	Hear	Feel	Modify
Look	Listen	Touch	Amend
View	Sound	Grasp	Experi
Appear	Tune in/out	Hold	Chang
Show	Quiet	Grip	Under s
Illuminate	Explain	Contact	Notice
Clear	Music	Solid	Percei
Hazy	Announce	Concrete	Consid
Foggy	Harmonise	Scrape	Learn
Picture	Shout	Throw	Think
Watch	Ask	Catch	Decide
Review	Question	Hard	Proces
Focus	Tell	Unfeeling	Teach
Brilliant	Rhythm	Turn	Aware
Imagine	Scream	Tap	Know
Visualise	Resonate	Sensation	Asses s

61

Instead of leading the client down the VAK path of description, the Auditory Digital words will enable you to question the client without providing an unconscious representational system answer. The client can then answer in their choice of representational systems.

The Immediate Care Process

Simon Maryan

LIST OF PREDICATE PHRASES

VISUAL	AUDITORY	KINAESTHETIC	AUDITORY DIGITAL
Look forward	That sounds good	Tap into	Logical reasons
See to it	Rings a bell	Touchyfeely	To my mind
Point of view	Falls on deaf ears	Get a handle on	The rationale is
I see your point	Hidden message	Let's make contact	Learn from this
Blind spot	Give me a call	Get to grips with	Makes sense
Light up	Sound asleep	Hold on	Makes no sense
Crystal clear	To tell the truth	Catch on	Change of mind

The Immediate Care Process

Clearcut	Word for word	Get in touch	Think ahead
Mind's eye	Tune In/Out	Touch base	Knows his mind
In view of	Voice an opinion	Smooth operator	Perception is reality

Tunnel Vision	Music to my ears	Scraping the barrel	To my way of thinking
Shortsighted	Loud and clear	Start from scratch	Process improvement
Mental image	Sound-effects	Lay our cards on the table	Modify our thinking
Focus in on	Give an earful	Kick some ideas around	Consider our options
Showing off	On the same wavelength	Throw some ideas around	Due consideration
Sight for sore eyes	Singing from the same hymn sheet	Pull some strings	Factual assessment

EXAMPLES OF PREDICATE PHRASES AT WORK

VISUAL

If I could *show* you an *attractive* way in which you could **<have whatever you want>,** you would at least want to *look* at it, wouldn't you? If this *looks good* to you we will go ahead and *focus* on getting the paperwork done.

AUDITORY

If I could discuss how to set up an account.

KINAESTHETIC

If I could help you *get hold of* a handling the paperwork.

AUDITORY DIGITAL

If I could process the account-opening.

COMBINATION

If I could help you *see* a discuss setting up an account.

Please note that the words in italics are for your benefit. They would not be stressed in speech nor italicised in writing. The above could apply to any business/work benefit, such as:

- reducing staff turnover
- improving efficiency/customer experience
- gaining market share

EYE ACCESSING CUES EYE PATTERN CHART

As You Look At a Normally Organised Person

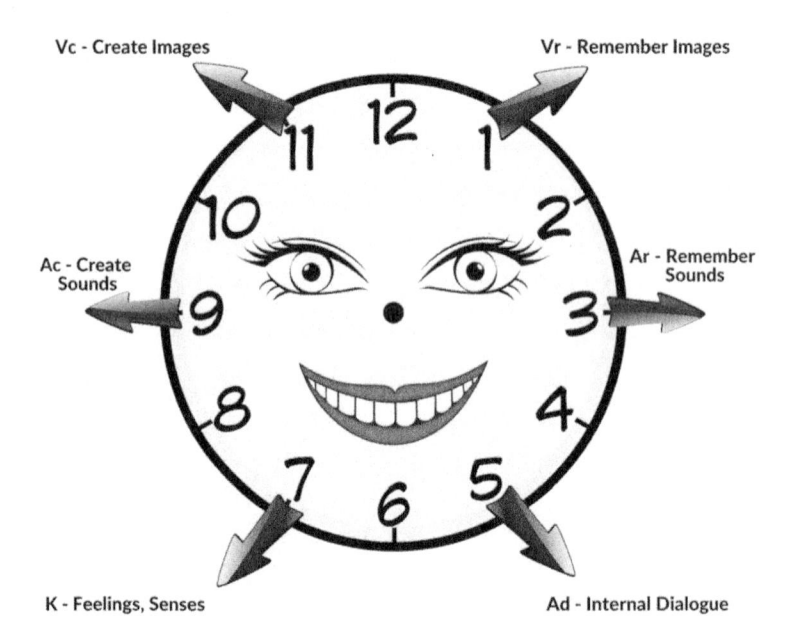

Vc - Create Images
Vr - Remember Images
Ac - Create Sounds
Ar - Remember Sounds
K - Feelings, Senses
Ad - Internal Dialogue

V^c = Visual Constructed - Images Never Seen Before

V^r = Visual Remembered/Recall - Seeing Images From Memory

A^c = Auditory Constructed - Making Up Sounds Not Heard Before

A^r = Auditory Remembered/Recall - Remembered Sounds Heard Before

K = Kinaesthetic - Feelings, Sense of Taste, Touch, Smell

A_d = Auditory Digital - Internal Dialogue or Recitation

ELICITATION OF EYE PATTERNS

Here is a **selection** of questions to ask in order to elicit whether someone is normally organised. Please ensure that you only ask questions that will require the client to access one representational system. Please use common sense and remember to ask questions that are likely to be un-intrusive.

V^r : Visual Remembered

What colour was the room you grew up in?

What colour was your first car/ bicycle?

What did your favourite toy look like when you were a young child?

What was your teacher/boss/partner wearing this morning?

What colour comes after Red on traffic lights?

V^c : Visual Constructed

What would your room (car) look like if it were blue?

What would your house look like overgrown with ivy?

What would your car look like with 50 helium balloons attached?

A^r : Auditory Remembered

What was the very last thing I said?

Remember the sound of your mother's/boss'/partner's voice?

What did your favourite song in school sound like?

A^c : Auditory Constructed

What would I sound like if I had Donald Duck's voice?

What would it sound like in an echo chamber?

What would your car horn be like if it sounded like a foghorn?

K: Kinaesthetic (feelings, sense of touch, taste, smell)

What does it feel like to put on wet socks?

What does it feel like to hold a baby?

Remember the feeling of walking along the beach barefoot?

What does your favourite food taste like?

A$_d$: Auditory Digital (internal dialogue)

Recite the Lord's Prayer to yourself?

What do you say to yourself when things go wrong/right?

Recite your three times table to yourself?

SOME TIPS FOR ELICITING EYE PATTERNS

- If eyes don't move, ask a more searching question
- De-focussing could mean that that someone is visualising
- Look to listen rule? (ie some people believe it is important to keep eye contact at all times). Look away a few times.
- Cultural aspects
- Remember, some people access very quickly – keep in uptime, observe
- Remember the distinction between 'Lead
- Representational System' and 'Primary
- Representational System'
- Ask questions that access only one representational system at a time
- Be sensitive to clients when asking questions.

EYE TRACKING EXERCISES

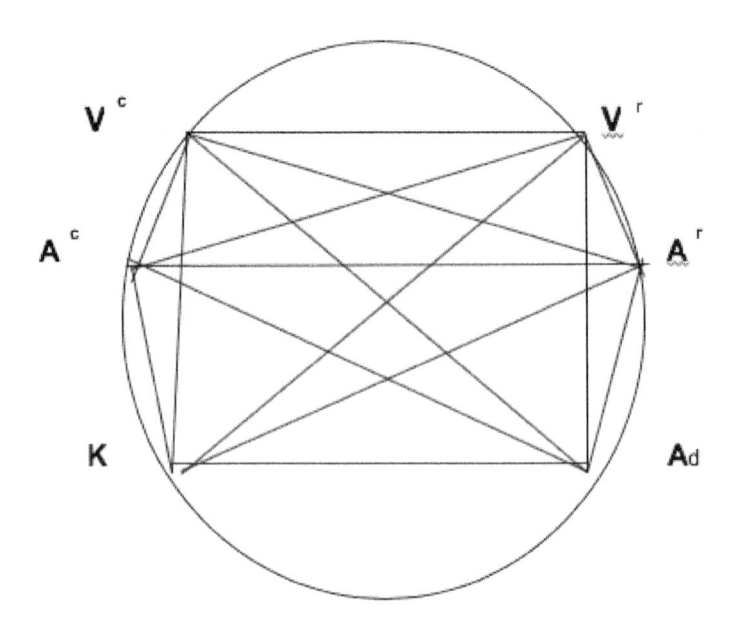

As the Practitioner:

- move your index finger **slowly** in a circle, clockwise and anti-clockwise.
- Move your finger from all 6 segments into the other 5 segments

- Watch the client's eyes. Notice any uneven movements (possibly a sign of a synesthesia), or if the client finds it difficult to move their eyes into a particular segment.

Client, notice which segment(s) are more difficult to move into, and keep your head still as you do this.

SUMMARY OF EYE ACCESSING CUES

The representational system we are using shows itself through our body language in our posture, breathing pattern, voice tone, and eye movements. These are known as **Accessing Cues**. They are associated with using the representational systems and make them easier to access.

This summary chart is from Joseph O'NLP Workbook:

	VISUAL	AUDITORY	KINAESTHETIC
Eye Movement	Defocused, or up to the right or left.	In the midline	Below the midline, usually to the left as you look at them
Voice Tone & Tempo	Generally rapid, speech, high, clear voice tone	Melodious tone, resonant at a medium pace. Often has an underlying rhythm.	Low and deep tonality often slow and soft, with many pauses.
Breathing	High, shallow breathing in the top part of the chest.	Even breathing in the middle part of the chest cavity.	Deeper breathing from the abdomen.
Posture &	More tension	Often medium	Rounded

| Gestures | in the body, often with the neck extended. Often thinner (ectomorphic) body type. | (mesomorphic) body type. There may be rhythmic movements of the body as if listening to music. Head may be tilted to the side in thought (in the 'telephone position'.) | shoulders, head down, relaxed muscle tone, may gesture to abdomen and midline. Often endomorphic body type. |

OVERLAPPING REPRESENTATIONAL SYSTEMS

Overlapping Representational Systems can be used to help a client to access their **least** preferred rep system by taking them from their most preferred system to their least preferred. For example, supposing a client says they have difficulty visualising, and use the kinaesthetic rep system easily and frequently. You could say something like "remember being on a beach, feeling the sand between your toes and the sun beating down on your skin (K), and notice the sounds of the children shouting, or the seagulls cooing, and the waves lapping against the shore (A), and as you hear that, notice what the people look like on the beach, see the yellow of the sand and the blue of the water (V)". **NB:** please ensure that you use examples that you know will be acceptable and ecological to the client.

Overlapping Representational Systems can also be used when a client is running a problem. Often, the modality or representational system of the stuck state is Kinaesthetic (Ki) and/or Auditory Digital (Ad). By pacing their problem state in K, it is possible to overlap their representational systems through Auditory Construct

(A^C) to Visual Construct (V^C), and so to the solution of their problem.

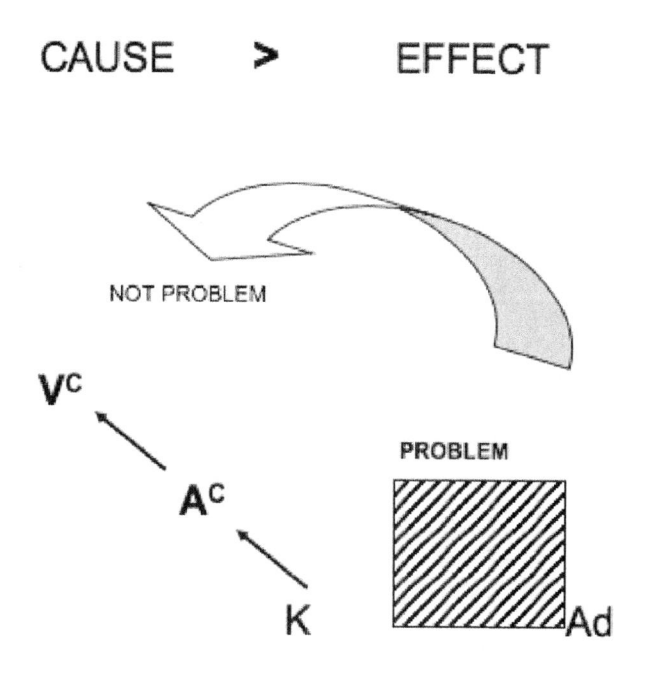

CAUSE > EFFECT

NOT PROBLEM

V^C

A^C

K

PROBLEM

Ad

SYNESTHESIA

There are two overall forms of synesthesia:

- projective synesthesia: people who see actual colours, forms, or shapes when stimulated (the widely understood version of synesthesia).

- associative synesthesia: people who feel a very strong and involuntary connection between the stimulus and the sense that it triggers. This is the most common form that we encounter

For example, in chromesthesia (sound to colou might hear a trumpet, and think very strongly that it sounds "orange.

Synesthesia can occur between nearly any two senses or perceptual modes and while nearly every logically possible combination of experiences can occur, several types are more common than others.

AUDITORY-TACTILE SYNESTHESIA

In **auditory-tactile synesthesia**, certain sounds can induce sensations in parts of the body. For example, someone with auditory-tactile synesthesia may experience that hearing a specific word feels like touch in one specific part of the body or may experience that certain sounds can create a sensation in the skin without being touched. It is one of the least common forms of synesthesia.

MISOPHONIA

Misophonia is a neurological disorder in which negative experiences (anger, fright, hatred, disgust) are triggered by specific sounds. Richard Cytowic suggests that misophonia is related to, or perhaps a variety of, synesthesia. Miren Edelstein and her colleagues have compared misophonia to synesthesia in terms of connectivity between different brain regions as well as specific symptoms. They formed the hypothesis that "a pathological distortion of connections between the auditory cortex and limbic structures could cause a form of sound-emotion synesthesia."

MIRROR-TOUCH SYNESTHESIA

This is a rare form of synesthesia where individuals feel the same sensation that another person feels (such as touch). For instance, when such a synesthete observes someone being tapped on their shoulder, the synesthete involuntarily feels a tap on their own shoulder as well. People with this type of synesthesia have been shown to have higher empathy levels compared to the general population. This may be related to the so-called mirror neurons present in the motor areas of the brain, which have also been linked to empathy.

LEXICAL-GUSTATORY SYNESTHESIA

This is another rare form of synesthesia where certain tastes are experienced when hearing words. For example, the word basketball might taste like waffles. The documentary 'Derek Tastes Of Earwax' gets its name from this phenomenon, in references to pub owner James Wannerton who experiences this particular sensation whenever he hears the name spoken. It is estimated that 0.2% of the population has this form of synesthesia.

OTHER FORMS

Other forms of synesthesia have been reported, but little has been done to analyse them scientifically. There are at least 80 different types of synesthesia.

In August 2017 a research article in the journal *Social Neuroscience* reviewed studies with fMRI to determine if persons who experience Autonomous Sensory Meridian Response are experiencing a form of synesthesia. While a determination has not yet been made, there is anecdotal evidence that this may be the case, based on significant and consistent differences from the control group, in terms of functional connectivity within neural pathways. It is unclear whether this will lead to ASMR being included as a form of existing synesthesia, or if a new type will be considered.

The following article is written by Marilyn McWilliams, Certified EFT Practitioner on Synesthesia in Veterans working through trauma.

https://www.eftuniverse.com/trauma-and-ptsd/eft-and-thegift-of-synesthesia

Simon Maryan

MODALITIES & SUBMODALITIES

Submodalities are the subsets, or finer distinctions of the or the Representational Systems by which we represent information through our five senses. They are the building blocks of the representational systems by which we code, order and give meaning to the experiences we have. Submodalities are how we structure our experiences, they are the 'brain's language'.

How do you know what you believe and what you do not believe? You code the two different kinds of beliefs in different submodalities. We create meaning by using different submodalities to code our experience, for example someone we like and someone we dislike. Changing submodalities is a very effective and powerful way of changing the meaning of an experience. When we set a goal, for example, the more attention we pay to the submodalities, the more specifically refined it becomes. The finer our distinctions, the more clearly and creatively we can design our future.

Some of our submodalities are as follows:

VISUAL SUBMODALITIES

Framed or Panoramic Near or Far

Flat or 3-Dimensional Clear or Fuzzy

Colour or Black & White Associated or Dissociated

Still or Moving Picture Large or Small Central Character

Bright or Dim Focused or Defocused

AUDITORY SUBMODALITIES

Volume Direction of Sound(s)

Pitch High / Low Duration of Sound(s)

Tempo Fast / Slow Regular or Irregular

Rhythm

Timbre / Quality Internal or External

KINAESTHETIC SUBMODALITIES

Feeling Internal / External Steady / Vibrating

Pressure Movement Fast / Slow

Smooth / Rough Shape

Hard / Soft Duration of Feeling

CRITICAL AND DRIVER SUBMODALITIES

Critical Submodalities are the submodalities that make a difference in the meaning of an experience. Some of the submodalities are more critical than others in defining our experiences. A **Driver** is a submodality that is so critical that it carries all the other submodality differences when we change it.

ANALOGUE AND DIGITAL SUBMODALITIES

Submodalities can be either . Analogue submodalities are those which have a wide range or spectrum, and digital submodalities are those which are either one thing or another.

Examples of analogue submodalities are size (a picture can be very big, tiny or anything in between), brightness (a picture can be very bright, very dim or anything in between), volume (a sound can be very loud, very soft or anything in between) and weight (heavy, light or in between). Examples of digital submodalities are Associated/dissociated, black & white or colour, 3d or flat. The distinction between analogue and digital submodalities becomes particularly important at Master Practitioner level.

ASSOCIATED AND DISSOCIATED

Usually one of the critical visual submodalities is Associated /

Dissociated. When we look through our own eyes, we are **Associated**. When we see our body in the picture, we are **Dissociated.**

Often, people will let you know the submodalities for a particular situation in everyday language, eg "I've got this big problem hanging over me" or "it's too close for comfort"

POSSIBLE USES OF SUBMODALITIES

Here are some of the many uses of submodalities:

- Create a change- like to dislike.
- People – making someone seem less intimidating eg: cold calling, meetings, presentations.
- Overcoming grief.
- Changing beliefs.
- Making something seem more appealing eg exercise, paperwork.
- Shifting the importance of values/criteria.
- Becoming more 'internally referenced' and better able to make decisions.
- Getting out of destructive situations– 'The Last Straw' Threshold pattern
- Motivation.
- Overcoming confusion.

The above list is by no means exhaustive!

For more information on submodalities, refer to the following books:

"Using Your Brain For A Change". Richard Bandler

"Change Your Mind And Keep The Change" – Steve Andreas,
Connirae Andreas

"An Insider's Guide to Submodalities" – Richard Bandler and
Will MacDonald

ELICITING SUBMODALITIES

Once you have determined which submodalities are the appropriate ones to use with a client, the first thing to do is to elicit the submodalities. Here are some tips:

- Do it quickly – the unconscious mind works quickly.
- Make sure that your attention is on the client and not just the submodality checklist. ●Ask 'do you have a picture?', 'are there any sounds?', 'are there any feelings?'
- Develop your own shorthand when noting the submodalities.

Use the chart on the next page for the upcoming exercises and aim to work quicker with each exercise.

USING SUBMODALITIES

There are three main types of Submodality intervention.

1. Alter Submodalities Individually – this is important when first learning

Having elicited the submodalities, make changes one by one, asking whether it makes the situation better/more desired, worse/less desired or no change. Continue until the client has his/her desired outcome.

2. Working With 'Drivers'

Drivers are the submodalities that make the most difference to someone's experience. Usually the driver will be a visual submodality, although this is not always the case – every person is unique.

One way to assist someone to find the driver is to follow method 1 above, and ask them to let you know which of the changes has the biggest impact. Sometimes you will be able to notice this from the way someone responds when they are making the submodality change you have asked them to make.

Once you have assisted someone to find their driver for a particular experience, you may want to assist them in finding out whether that driver is the same across other contexts (food, drink, people, activities etc), or whether other submodalities are drivers in different contexts.

3. Contrastive Analysis/Mapping Across

Contrastive Analysis is comparing and contrasting submodalities of different states or two different Internal Representations with each other and finding the critical submodalities.

Mapping Across is discovering the drivers and then changing the submodalities of one Internal Representation to the other.

As we know, you can alter behaviour by altering state. The following is the process:

- **Identify the Two Responses/ Situations/States (or Values/Beliefs) That You Want to Contrast** — one undesired, one desired.
- **Elicit the submodalities of each.**
- **Do the Contrastive Analysis** - Determine the Critical Submodalities.
- **Map Across** - Change the submodalities of the current undesired state to those of the desired.
(This makes the person's response to/interpretation of the current undesired

situation the same as that of the desired situation).
Lock in the changes.
- **Test and Future Pace.** Future pacing is mentally going out into the future or rehearsing an outcome to ensure that the desired behaviour will occur.

SUBMODALITY EXERCISES

Exercise 1 – Making it even better

The purpose of this exercise is for the client to identify which submodality(ies) have the most positive impact.

1. Client thinks of a pleasant experience, a '7 out of 10' (where 10 is highest).
2. Practitioner elicits the submodalities
3. Practitioner takes each submodality one **at a time** to find out which one(s) make the most difference:

i. Starting with visual submodalities, ask the client to change the submodality to the opposite (e.g. 'colour' to 'black & white')

ii. ask the client whether that makes it better, worse or no change, and **whatever the reply, ask the client to return it to how it was**. Make a note of the ones that make it better
(i.e. increase the score)

iii. If the submodality is analogue, move it first in one direction, and **if that makes it worse**, ask the client to bring it back to how it was and then to move it in

the opposite direction. (e.g., if 'near', make it 'far', and then 'even nearer'.
1. Do as many of the submodalities as time permits – at least all of the visuals.
2. Discuss with the client which one(s) made the biggest impact. Ideally find the one which makes the biggest positive difference.
3. Test by asking the client to change just that one submodality. The client may choose to keep the change(s) if he/she wishes to increase the score.

Exercise 2 – Making Changes

The purpose of the exercise is to use submodalities to change the client's response to the situation.

As Exercise 1 above, except:

1. Client thinks of a relatively minor 'challenge', or something they are not looking forward to (e.g. a particular work meeting), a '3 out of 10' (where 10 is better). Practitioner does the 'pre-intervention questions' and ecology check.
2. In steps 3ii and 3iii, if the change made improves the situation, keep it.
3. Check in with the client every 2-3 changes to ask the score. Once you've reached the target score, ask the client to 'lock in the changes'.
4. After that, future pace.

TIPS FOR SUCCESSFUL SUBMODALITY INTERVENTIONS

1. Elicit quickly – faster than the client's conscious mind would like you to process.

   i. Find the drivers, the key submodalities
   ii. We can use the submodalities of a universal experience where appropriate to shift someone's experience. A t had the experience they will go inside and make it up. Examples are:
      - knowing that the sun will rise tomorrow – something that is absolutely true.
      - how we respond to a red traffic light or green traffic light – an automatic response.
      - a belief no longer true (Father Christmas),

Additional Tips

- Use the submodalities checklist until you can recall the main submodalities, in particular the visual, off by heart.

- If you need to work quickly, just use the visual submodalities, and then ask 'are there any sounds that are important?' and 'are there any feelings that are important?'.

MEMORY & THE LIMBIC SYSTEM

Why it is useful to know how your brain works and how you remember and learn things?

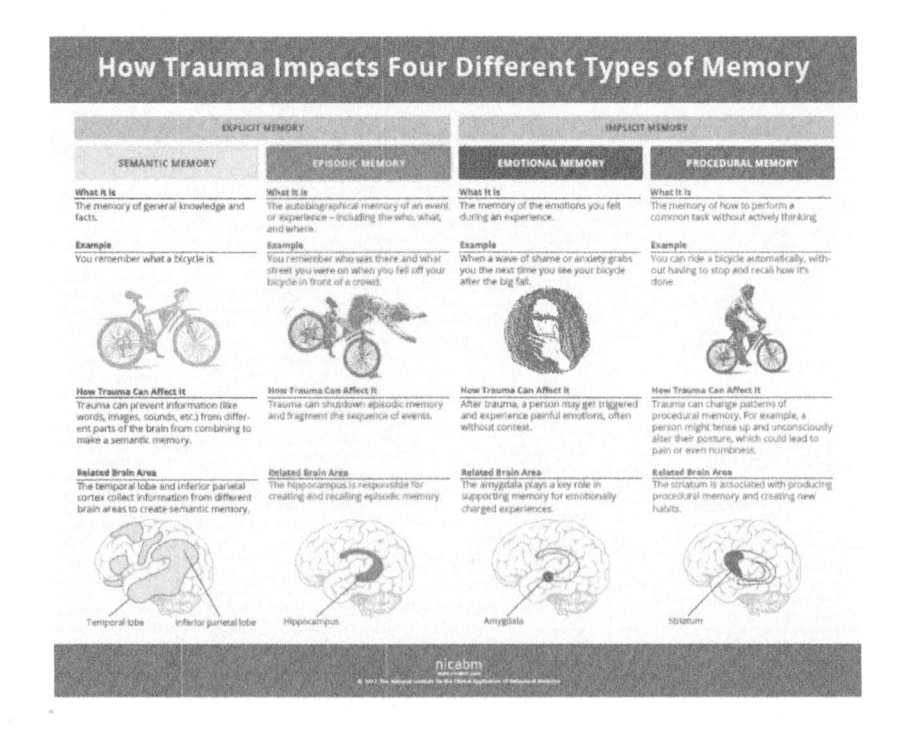

How Trauma Impacts Four Different Types of Memory

	EXPLICIT MEMORY		IMPLICIT MEMORY	
	SEMANTIC MEMORY	**EPISODIC MEMORY**	**EMOTIONAL MEMORY**	**PROCEDURAL MEMORY**
What It Is	The memory of general knowledge and facts.	The autobiographical memory of an event or experience – including the who, what, and where.	The memory of the emotions you felt during an experience.	The memory of how to perform a common task without actively thinking
Example	You remember what a bicycle is.	You remember who was there and what street you were on when you fell off your bicycle in front of a crowd.	When a wave of shame or anxiety grabs you the next time you see your bicycle after the big fall.	You can ride a bicycle automatically, without having to stop and recall how it's done.
How Trauma Can Affect It	Trauma can prevent information (like words, images, sounds, etc.) from different parts of the brain from combining to make a semantic memory.	Trauma can shutdown episodic memory and fragment the sequence of events.	After trauma, a person may get triggered and experience painful emotions, often without context.	Trauma can change patterns of procedural memory. For example, a person might tense up and unconsciously alter their posture, which could lead to pain or even numbness.
Related Brain Area	The temporal lobe and inferior parietal cortex collect information from different brain areas to create semantic memory.	The hippocampus is responsible for creating and recalling episodic memory.	The amygdala plays a key role in supporting memory for emotionally charged experiences.	The striatum is associated with producing procedural memory and creating new habits.
	Temporal lobe / Inferior parietal lobe	Hippocampus	Amygdala	Striatum

nicabm

We all remember information, even when we are not trying to and that is the most effective way to do it, not try too hard. When we understand how we learn best we can then recreate the circumstances we each need in order to remember most effectively.

Our brains store information in a variety of locations, however the particular types of memory we are looking at here are located deep in our brains and are attached to the brain stem.

They are at the core of who we are.

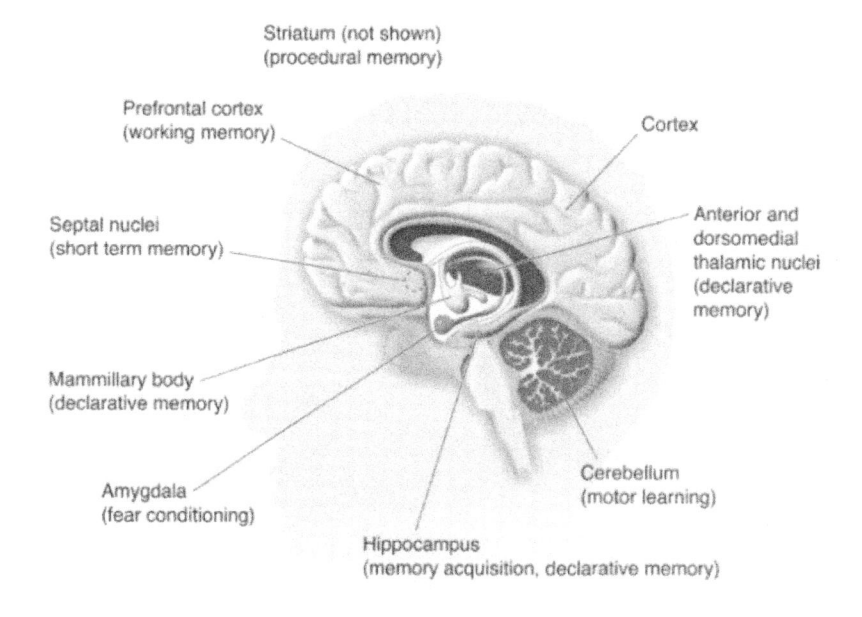

Striatum (not shown)
(procedural memory)

Prefrontal cortex
(working memory)

Cortex

Septal nuclei
(short term memory)

Anterior and dorsomedial thalamic nuclei
(declarative memory)

Mammillary body
(declarative memory)

Amygdala
(fear conditioning)

Cerebellum
(motor learning)

Hippocampus
(memory acquisition, declarative memory)

The following 2 images provide visuals to demonstrate this.

SUBMODALITY TRACKING WORKSHEET LIMBIC SYSTEM OVERVIEW PERCEPTUAL BLINDNESS & CONSCIOUS OVERLOAD

Our Conscious minds (explicit memory) can only deal with a certain amount of information at any one time and this is also affected by various elements.

We can handle between 5 & 9 bits of information in our conscious, explicit memory

Our conscious minds work like a conveyor belt and when we have between 5-9 bits of information in our minds our short term memory is full. Our conscious mind does not discriminate between what is needed and what isn't, all it does is drop a bit of information off the end of the conveyor to make room for the new bit. This bit of information that just dropped out could be something that you need to remember such as that you left your wallet on the restaurant table, or you left your front door unlocked.

What Affects Memory

- Stress
- Disease
- Having a busy mind
- Lack of sleep
- Alcohol
- Trauma – psychological and physical
- Body position

- Body's response to external stimulus
- Autonomic Nervous System – Limbic System (Emotion)
- Sympathetic Nervous System (SNS) – Fight or Flight (Implicit)
- Parasympathetic Nervous System (PNS) – Promotes relaxation (Explicit)
- Somatic Nervous System – Sensory input : external/internal – processing & encoding information

Simon Maryan

BRAIN ACTIVITY AND BRAINWAVES

We've all experienced that magical feeling of being hit with 'a brainwave'. That moment of new-found clarity, a shift in perspective or a novel idea. And typically, it seems to appear out of nowhere. In between sips of coffee, while out for a walk, or simply indulging your dog in a good belly rub.

While "a brainwave" can be a figure of speech to describe our thoughts, scientists and clinicians can use literal brainwaves, measured on the head, to help understand the functioning of the human brain. As it turns out, the key to having more of these

'aha' moments lies in understanding the science behind brainwaves. Neuroscientists have been studying brainwaves – the popular name for the field of electroencephalography – for nearly a century.

WHAT ARE BRAINWAVES?

The brain has billions of neurons, and each individual neuron connects (on average) to thousands of others. Communication happens between them through small electrical currents that travel along the neurons and throughout enormous networks of brain circuits. When all these neurons are activated they produce electrical pulses – visualise a wave rippling through the crowd at a sports arena – this synchronised electrical activity results in a "brainwave".

When many neurons interact in this way at the same time, this activity is strong enough to be detected even outside the brain. By placing electrodes on the scalp, this activity can be amplified, analysed, and visualised. This is electroencephalography, or EEG – a fancy word that just means electric brain graph. (Encephalon, the brain, is derived from the ancient Greek "enképhalos," meaning within the head.)

One way that EEG 'brainwaves' convey information is in their rate of repetition. Some oscillations, measured on the scalp, occur at more than 30 cycles per second (and up to 100 cycles per second!) These cycles, also called frequencies, are measured as Hz, or hertz, after the scientist who proved the existence of electromagnetic waves.

When looked at this way, brainwaves come in five flavours, each of which corresponds to a Greek letter. As we'll see, these different brainwaves correspond to different states of thought or experience. While there are many other ways to analyse brainwaves, many practitioners of a field called neuro-feedback rely on dividing brain oscillations into these five categories. Some of these brain oscillations are more easily detectable on specific parts of the scalp, corresponding to the parts of the brain just below. The brain has many specialised regions which correspond to different processes, thoughts, and sensations. Particular oscillations often reflect distinct regions and networks in the brain communicating with each other.

THE 5 MAIN TYPES OF BRAINWAVES

Different patterns of brainwaves can be recognised by their amplitudes and frequencies. Brainwaves can then be categorised based on their level of activity or frequency. It's important to remember, though, that brainwaves are not the source or the cause of brain states, or of our experiences of our own minds – they're just some of the detectable reflections of the complex processes in the brain that produce our experience of being, thinking, and perceiving.

- **Slow activity** refers to a lower frequency and high amplitude (the distance between two peaks of a wave). These oscillations are often much larger in amplitude (wave depth). Think: low, the deep beat of a drum.
- **Fast activity** refers to a higher frequency and often smaller amplitude. Think: high pitched flute.

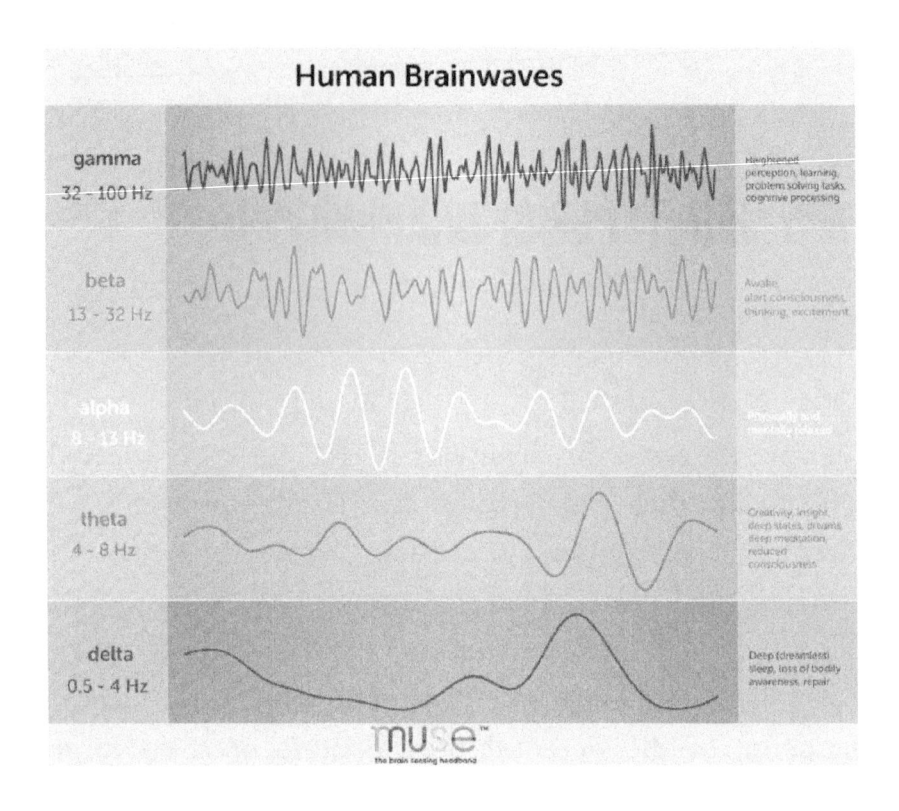

Below are five often-described brainwaves, from fastest activity levels to slowest.

GAMMA BRAINWAVES

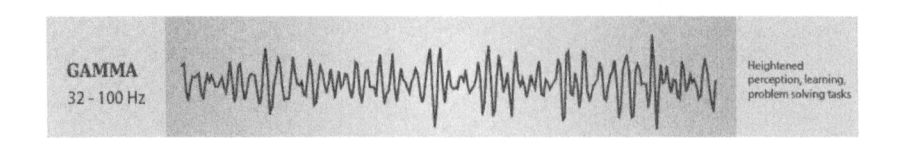

- Frequency: 32 – 100 Hz
- Associated state: Heightened perception, learning, problem-solving tasks

Gamma brainwaves are the fastest measurable EEG brainwaves, and have been equated to 'heightened perception', or a 'peak mental state' when there is simultaneous processing of information from different parts of the brain. Gamma brainwaves have been observed to be much stronger and more regularly observed in very long-term meditators including Buddhist

Monks.

BETA BRAINWAVES

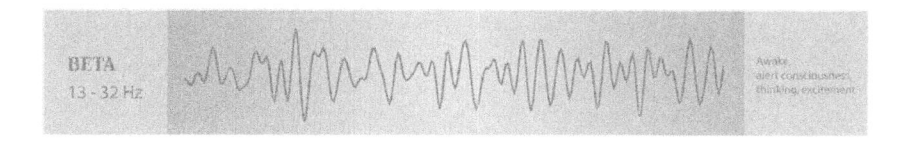

- Frequency: 13-32 Hz
- State: Alert, normal alert consciousness, active thinking For example:
- Active conversation
- Making decisions
- Solving a problem
- Focusing on a task
- Learning a new concept

Beta brainwaves are easiest to detect when we're busy thinking actively.

ALPHA BRAINWAVES

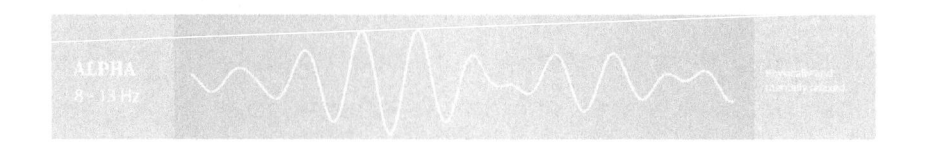

- Frequency: 8-13 Hz
- State: Physically and mentally relaxed

Alpha brainwaves are some of the most easily observed and were the first to be discovered. They become detectable when the eyes are closed and the mind is relaxed. They can also often be found during activities such as:

- Hypnosis
- Meditating
- Yoga
- Just before falling asleep
- Being creative and artistic

THETA BRAINWAVES

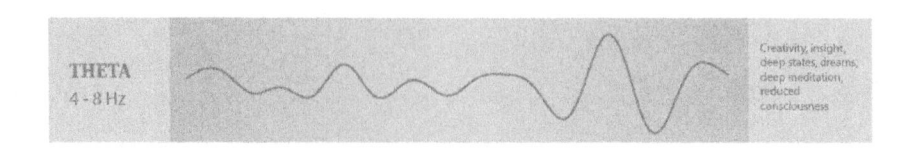

- Frequency: 4-8 Hz

- State: Creativity, insight, dreams, reduced consciousness

According to Professor Jim Lagopoulos of Sydney University, "previous studies have shown that theta waves indicate deep relaxation and occur more frequently in highly experienced meditation practitioners. The source is probably frontal parts of the brain, which are associated with monitoring of other mental processes."

Most frequently, theta brainwaves are strongly detectable when we're dreaming in our sleep (think, the movie Inception), but they can also be seen during :

- Deep meditation
- Daydreaming

When we're doing a task that is so automatic that the mind can disengage from it e.g. brushing teeth, showering. Research has also shown a positive association of theta waves with memory, creativity and psychological well-being. (5) (6)

DELTA BRAINWAVES

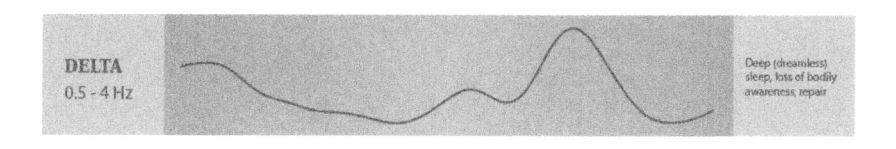

DELTA
0.5 - 4 Hz

Deep (dreamless) sleep, loss of bodily awareness, repair

- Frequency: 0.5-4 Hz
- State: Deep restorative sleep, dream

These are the slowest of all brainwaves, and are strongest when we are enjoying restorative sleep in a dreamless state. This is also the state where healing and rejuvenation are stimulated, which is why it's so crucial to get enough sleep each night.

INFLUENCES ON YOUR STATE OF MIND

States of Mind – Attitude: Beliefs & Emotions

"Beliefs are translated into attitudes through values. Our beliefs and values impact on our Attitude and in turn our behaviour."

Attitudes are long lasting patterns of feelings and beliefs about other people, ideas, or objects that are based in people's experiences and shape their future behaviour.

Attitudes are usually evaluative. Attitudes are formed early in life through learning processes. An attitude is learned and our actions are related to it. We have a choice as to what attitude to adopt.

Attitude Drives Behaviour: Our body language is a result of our mental attitude. By choosing our attitude we create a certain mood and send out a message that everyone understands, consciously and/or unconsciously.

Attitudes are typically related to liking/disliking or with a positive/negative bias. They are more than personality traits, but linguistically used interchangeably if the traits are substantially broad or temperament-like.

What influences your state of mind?

Your state of mind changes from day to day and throughout the day depending on how you respond emotionally to what is happening around you and to you. This creates your mood and this influences your attitude to work, people and situations.

How others behave towards you and speak to you influences your mood and your attitude through the way that you respond emotionally to that interaction.

EMOTIONAL RESPONSE VS DECISIONS

When an event prompts an emotional reaction, the sympathetic nervous system mobilises the body for an adaptive fight-or-flight response.

Fight-or-Flight

Emotional Response vs Decisions

Mapping Amygdala Hijacking
(Fight-or-Flight Response)

Thalamus

Reasoned Response

Fight-or-Flight Response

Stimulus

Response

Visual Cortex

Amygdala

Electro-chemical stimulants that produce emotional response

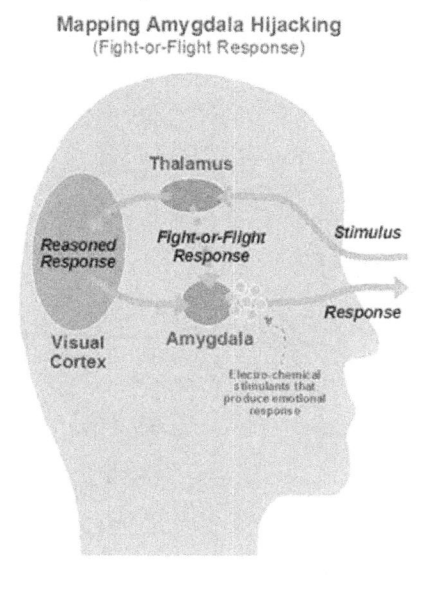

The Visual Cortex is sometimes called the "air traffic controller" of the brain. The Thalamus routes the bulk of the information of the cortex (as illustrated on the previous page, to the visual cortex as the stimulus is visual), and a small amount of the information to the **Amygdala (the emotional response centre – regulator of our emotions).**

The Amygdala is most commonly associated with the emotions of fear and anxiety. When no immediate threat is perceived, the cortex develops a reasoned response which is then routed to the amygdala for generating motivation and action through the release of a suitable amount of electro-chemicals (shown as small circles). **If a threat is perceived, however, the amygdala can "hijack" the reasoned response process and flood the brain with electro-chemicals for generating a fast "fight-or-flight" type response.**

Such a response can save our lives in certain situations, or get us into trouble by overreacting in other situations (our "hot buttons" get pushed), leading to angry words or sometimes violence etc.

We all have certain triggers – things that cause us to have an emotional reaction and trigger our innate — fight or flight response. This limits our capacity to think clearly and causes us to move to default behaviours that may not be skilful or effective. Here are some default behaviours you might see (and experience yourself!)

- Someone gets defensive when they feel criticised – **feedback**
- Avoiding difficult conversations - **redundancy, firing, disciplinary**
- A person gives in to a strongly worded demand when they really don't want to – f**ear, bullying, intimidation**
- Someone becomes controlling and directive when they are feeling overwhelmed
- A person shuts down and becomes quiet when there is conflict in a meeting

These above examples of emotional reactions can force us into un-skilful default behaviours.

Emotional Response vs Decisions

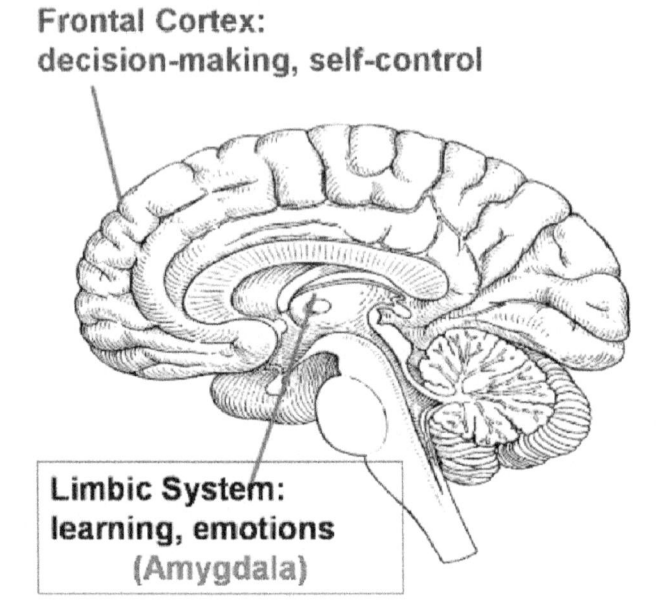

Frontal Cortex:
decision-making, self-control

Limbic System:
learning, emotions
(Amygdala)

Our default response and Pavlovian thinking. Pavlovian thinking is somewhat insidious because we can't see ourselves doing this. We think we are thinking about our own reflexive actions but even as the more evolved parts of the brain are witnessing these Pavlovian responses, we are totally unable to control the reptilian' parts of the brain. So, the mind is forced mindlessly to follow a set track engraved by the Amygdala which overrides all other systems.

When we try to override the Amygdala's systems of default response, we cause **EMOTIONAL DISTRESS**. Even as the forebrain frantically forces the rest of the brain to do as it says, the emotional toll can be tremendous and often, too painful, so we give up and yield to the set systems of the inner brain.

3 critical 'performance levers' that need be used:

- Behavioural change happens mostly by engaging a person's emotions and feelings.
- What we perceive defines what we believe. And this belief or perception is what guides our behaviour. Behaviour often has a large impact in learning/performance environments due to the influence of behaviourism.
- Values are one of the components of attitudes. Values help to determine how we will act as they help us to weigh the importance of various alternatives. They drive all organisational and individual efforts.

SOME KEY LEARNING POINTS:

- People view the past through the Amygdala's learning systems. It is not a logical progression but an EMOTIONAL one.
- The brains amygdala is the emotional triggerpoint for our decisions and actions (our behaviour). We base our decisions on emotional rather than rational responses to stimuli. People therefore need to ensure any persuasion requests to change are directed to the amygdala.

- Emotions control thinking. Every time a decision is made, we subconsciously call upon an emotional memory, a FEELING that will help guide us. It is important that you learn how to get in contact with your emotions - your **SELF GUIDANCE SYSTEM**.
- When we are able to activate our amygdala triggers, we can preclude any laborious rational thinking that can at best only engender very short-term change.

Note:

Imagining an alternative outcome, other than what actually occurred, can affect the emotions people experience and how they feel.

BELIEFS

Definition: A belief is a Driver (usually Unconscious) we hold and deeply trust about something. They can trigger our Values, Emotions & Behaviours. Beliefs tend to be buried deep within the subconscious. We seldom question beliefs; we hold them to be truths.

A Belief is aroused by an Activating Event e.g. without being aware of it, Jay held the belief that it was ok to openly criticise people. Alienation of his friends caused him to identify, question, and change this belief about what is acceptable to others

We each behave as though our beliefs are true. What we perceive defines what we believe and this belief or perception is what guides our behaviour. A Belief is a form of judging something to be true, intermediate between mere opinion and knowledge. Opinion is a subjective statement or thought about an issue or topic, and is the result of emotion or interpretation of facts.

Knowledge is learnt expertise, skills, facts and information.

A simple definition for belief is: A belief is an assumed truth. We create beliefs to anchor our understanding of the world around us and thus, once we have formed a belief, we will tend to persevere with that belief.

Change begins with awareness. Awareness begins with learning about how beliefs and emotional reaction are created by choice.

Some fundamental information about beliefs:

- May or may not be based on truth
- Can also be easily formed out of emotion relating to one or many incidents
- May or may not be supported by irrefutable evidence
- Usually have an emotional attachment, which strengthens belief
- Do not update themselves automatically and therefore are stored at the initial stage (emotional state, etc.)

3 Basic Types of Beliefs

1. **Casual Beliefs:** Everyday, practical beliefs that don't matter much if we get them wrong such as - I believe it will rain tomorrow
2. **Conditioned Beliefs:** These come from an assessment of what has happened in the past and then predicts the same results in the future. So we get beliefs such as I'm no good at this or I can't do

that. These beliefs, if negative, can stifle our potential and limit our lives.
3. **Core Beliefs:** Can be positive or negative, lead us to be an optimist or pessimist and decide the answers to such questions as Who am I?, What is life about? What we learn and experience in early life shapes beliefs about the world and ourselves. Core beliefs are like a mental framework that supports our thoughts, beliefs, values and perception. Core beliefs are the deepest of all because what we believe "deep down inside" underpins our value system and our attitudes and opinions. This is one of the reasons why core beliefs are seldom questioned even when they are causing enormous problems within the person who holds that core belief.

IDENTIFYING LIMITING BELIEFS

Beliefs we have that limit the way we live, or from being, doing or having what we want, are called **Limiting Beliefs**. They fall into five main categories:

1. Any 'feelings' that you can't feel: If the description you give yourself or someone else gives you which, when you "try it on," is something you cannot feel without hallucinating substantially. Eg 'I feel I have to worry'. Also, where the word 'feel' could be replaced by 'believe' and the sentence still makes sense, then that could indicate a limiting belief. Eg 'I feel (*believe*) people don't like me'.

Negations: Anytime there is a negation describing anything, which might be an emotion eg 'I'm not clever', 'I can't have a good relationship'

Comparatives: Whenever there are comparisons. Eg 'I'm not good enough', 'I can't make enough money/friends'

2. Limiting Decisions: Whenever a Limiting Belief is adopted, a Limiting Decision preceded that acceptance. A Limiting Decision preceded even the beliefs that were adopted from other people. Eg 'I should know all the answers', 'I should get it right every time'.

3. Modal Operators of Necessity: Words such as *have to, got to, must, ought, should.*

Some examples of Limiting Beliefs are as follows:

I must stay the way I don't want to be because

I can't get what I want because

I'll never get better because

My biggest problem is because

I'll always have this problem because

I don't deserve because

I'm not good enough to

NB. It is important to distinguish between statements of fact/truth, and limiting beliefs, for example:

POSSIBLE TRUTH/FACT LIMITING DECISION I don't have any money. I can't make any money.

I am not a good athlete. I cannot become a good athlete.

I don't have any qualifications. I need qualifications to succeed.

I don't trust people. People are not trustworthy.

THE EXTENDED LOGICAL LEVELS OF CHANGE

Introduction

The logical level is comprised of two dimensions. This extended model has been developed by Robert Dilts in conjunction with the Co-Founders of lli, Logical Levels Inventory - an online behavioural profiling tool, over the last 12 years.

The Extended Logical Levels Model

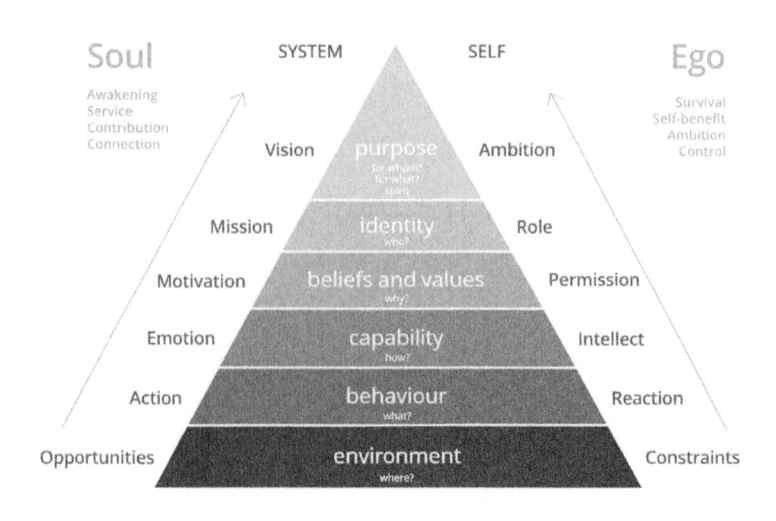

Soul	SYSTEM	SELF	Ego
Awakening			Survival
Service			Self-benefit
Contribution			Ambition
Connection	Vision / purpose (for whom? for what? spirit) / Ambition		Control
	Mission / identity (who?) / Role		
Motivation	beliefs and values (why?)	Permission	
Emotion	capability (how?)	Intellect	
Action	behaviour (what?)	Reaction	
Opportunities	environment (where?)	Constraints	

126

ENVIRONMENT

This level involves the specific external conditions in which our behaviours and interactions occur.

Environment is that which we perceive as being 'outside' of us. Environmental factors thus determine the external opportunities or constraints which individuals and organisations must recognise and to which they must respond.

The way we perceive the external environment is primarily related to the information we take in through our senses.

An individual relates to his or her environment in many ways. One important orientation is around the opportunities and constraints that exist in the environment.

OPPORTUNITY

This style involves seeing the opportunities, connections and possibilities that there are in the environment. Rules and boundaries may be stretched in the quest to even be creative.

However, they may lack focus and can over-promise. People with this style may be seen as optimistic and at the extreme as risk takers. When problems arise, they are more likely to see the opportunities that present themselves.

At work, people with this style may question the status quo but can be seen by some as mavericks.

If asked, they are able to put forward many of the benefits associated with a course of action and are often seen as enthusiastic in the promotion of new ideas and activities.

CONSTRAINTS

Cautious and careful embody the constraints style. Boundaries, guidelines and rules provide a sense of order and comfort and offer a defined space to work within. Within the defined space they may be willing to explore options but are more likely scanning for problems, threats or dangers.

As such they may appear resistant to new ideas and could be seen by some as negative. They will tend to identify those things that they want to avoid and may in the extreme appear obstinate and awkward.

People with this style may be prevented from doing things by factors in their environment and they may blame factors they see as being outside their control as reasons for not doing something.

At work they can see why ideas might not work and are able to point out the weak points in a plan or course of action. This style of thinking helps to avoid missing problems in advance, which otherwise might leave one under-prepared for difficulties.

BEHAVIOUR

This senses.

Our behaviours are the actions and reactions through which we interact with the people and the environment around us. The specific behaviours people actively engage in, such as talking, listening, thinking and doing, serve as the primary means for the successful achievement of desired goals and outcomes.

The dimension of action and reaction relates to the describes an important orientation of an individual to that level.

ACTION

This style resolve issues or at least think that they are.

These people are often dynamic and think, talk and walk fast. They are often the movers and shakers or agitators within a group or place of work.

Inactivity can be frustrating for people with this style and they can become bored. In extreme cases, they may be seen as insensitive – wanting to bulldoze decisions and ideas into action.

At work they tend to take the initiative and lead teams, or organisations and they are happy to bring about change in an organisation.

REACTION

This style describes people who wait for others or wait until the situation is right before taking action.

They prefer to respond to requests rather than initiating them and may shy away from work that puts them in charge of making decisions or taking the lead. People with a reaction style will respond once they have received an external stimulus.

The speed and nature of the response will vary according to other factors. (For example, from a knee jerk reaction through to almost never-ending analysis). People with this style sometimes report not feeling in control of their own destiny and would prefer others to improve their world.

At work, people with this style will usually be less decisive and enjoy taking requests. They are do.

CAPABILITY

This level relates to the inner maps and knowledge that lead to success. Our capabilities direct how behaviour is selected and monitored.

Many of our behaviours come from 'inner maps' and other into tangible behaviours.

An individual's orientation towards their capabilities in both emotional and intellectual intelligence is explored at this level.

INTELLECT

This style looks at the way people use their capabilities to organise their behaviours in an intellectual way. People with this style develop their capacity for rationale and intelligent thought.

They will often have a wide range of intellectual interests and abilities. People with this style will be filtering for specific facts and basic concepts and will be able to store and recall this information when required.

They will seek to understand things by organising, comparing and interpreting facts and ideas. They will make judgements about information, ideas or quality of work based on a set of criteria.

At work these people provide intellectual rigour to any debate through their use of rationale and logical thought.

EMOTION

This style looks at the way people use their capabilities to manage themselves and their relationships. People with this style are aware of their emotions, show more empathy and are more expression. People with this style are likely to be better adjusted emotionally, more popular, and more sensitive. They are usually approachable, listening to what people say, picking up their concerns and responding appropriately.

Skilled people with this style are good at establishing rapport and managing others. They are able to manage their emotions and impulses and act in a way that is appropriate to the situation.

BELIEFS AND VALUES

Our beliefs and values are the guiding principles that allow us to make meaning of the world and give us direction in our lives. They filter our perceptions of the environment and shape our communication with ourselves.

particular plans, maps and ways of thinking.

They relate to why we think and act as we lives.

The Oxford English dictionary defines a value as 'the worth, desirability or utility of a thing or the qualities on which these depend'. Robert Dilts says "because they are associated with worth, meaning and desire values are a primary source of (impetus) in people's lives. When peoples' values are met or matched, they feel a sense of satisfaction, harmony or rapport. When their values arc not met or matched, they often feel dissatisfied, violated or incongruent".

Values are intimately connected to beliefs. Beliefs are the cognitive structures which connect values to other aspects of our experience.

The dimension of motivation/permission describes one way that an individual is orientated around beliefs and values.

MOTIVATION

This style involves viewing the world in a way that means that a person is motivated or driven by desire, choice or possibility. People with this style will tend to be self-motivated and will evaluate events on the basis of what they feel is appropriate. They may gather information from others, but they usually make their own decisions.

People with this style will tend to focus on what they can do or want to do. They will tend to believe that they have a lot of control over their lives and will be encouraged to make decisions and take action to achieve their desires.

They are usually able to take feedback at the orders as information. They often have lots of motivation and drive but can sometimes be disappointed or frustrated if they have failed to achieve their desire.

PERMISSION

People with this style are likely to operate within the rules they have created either consciously or unconsciously. These will not primarily be the internal rules. These rules come from others where 'others' might include a variety of sources e.g. people in authority, parents and religious edicts.

They will tend to be motivated by what they ought to do and limited by what they are not allowed to confirm their own thoughts and decisions and

are likely to be more risk averse. In the extreme, their beliefs about obligations may put them under pressure and they may also have feelings of shame or guilt associated with them.

People with this style will tend to look at their life as something that is given and that they have little choice about. They will tend to hear information as internal thoughts of 'should', 'ought', 'can't', and 'mustn't'.

IDENTITY

Robert Dilts defines identity as our ability to relate to our sense of who we are. He states that our true identity is the totality of our potential (our 'super-position').

Our potential becomes limited when we confuse who we are with some part of what we into a single system. Our sense of identity also relates to our perception of ourselves in relation to the larger systems of which we are part, determining our sense of 'role' and 'mission'.

describes one way that an individual is orientated around identity.

MISSION

This style describes the way people think and feel about themselves which is more than just a role.

People with this style will be aware that the roles they take on in life are simply that and these roles do not define them. Their sense of self comes from a deeper connection with the unique personality with which they were born. They recognise that they have their own special way of being in the world which is conform.

People with this style are likely to be interested in and driven to find out more about themselves - to increase their understand how they relate to the larger systems of which they are a part. They will be more concerned with how they are rather than what they do in any actions they take. They are less likely to conform to fads or fashions.

People with this style are more likely to spend time reflecting ambiguities of life; they are therefore flexible towards new challenges and situations.

ROLE

This style carer, a parent, a director.

People will invariably have more than one role which they move between, either consciously or unconsciously, and each role has its own 'package' of beliefs, capabilities and behaviour. The roles people identify with are usually created without conscious choice.

They will use these roles to develop and maintain their sense of self. It is usually also important for people that the behaviours they display within each role are consistent with the image associated with that role.

Labels, status and titles are likely to be important to the extent they are connected with current or desired role.

The term 'role' as level of adaptability.

PURPOSE

Robert Dilts defines spirituality as "the subjective experience of being part of a larger system or field". This level looks at the way we perceive this field and the elements within it; be they people, objects or places and our connection to them. The questions that arise at this for?' and 'what's my purpose?'

The dimension of vision/ambition describes one way that an individual relates to his or her purpose.

VISION

People with this style feel a sense of connection with any larger system they believe themselves to be part of, for example family, nation, religion, company or humanity. They have a vision of how they want the larger system to be and may or may not know the part they play in this. If they do know the part they play this will tend to guide and direct the decisions and actions they take.

People with this style do not need to be recognised for their personal achievements nor are they driven by any need for achievement for self. They are motivated in the achievement of the bigger picture. They are not concerned about the vision being achieved in their lifetime.

AMBITION

People with this style feel a sense of connection to what they want to achieve. They may have more than one ambition for different areas of their life and also at different stages of their life. Any of their ambitions will provide guidance and meaning for the actions and decisions taken.

As one ambition is achieved it is likely that it will be followed by the creation of a new ambition. People with this style tend to create a connection with their future self through their ambition.

PERSONAL EXPLORATION EXERCISE

The purpose of this exercise is to enhance alignment and gain clarity. It can be used by individuals or groups, and can be used for a variety of contexts. This has been adapted from the original exercise created by Robert Dilts.

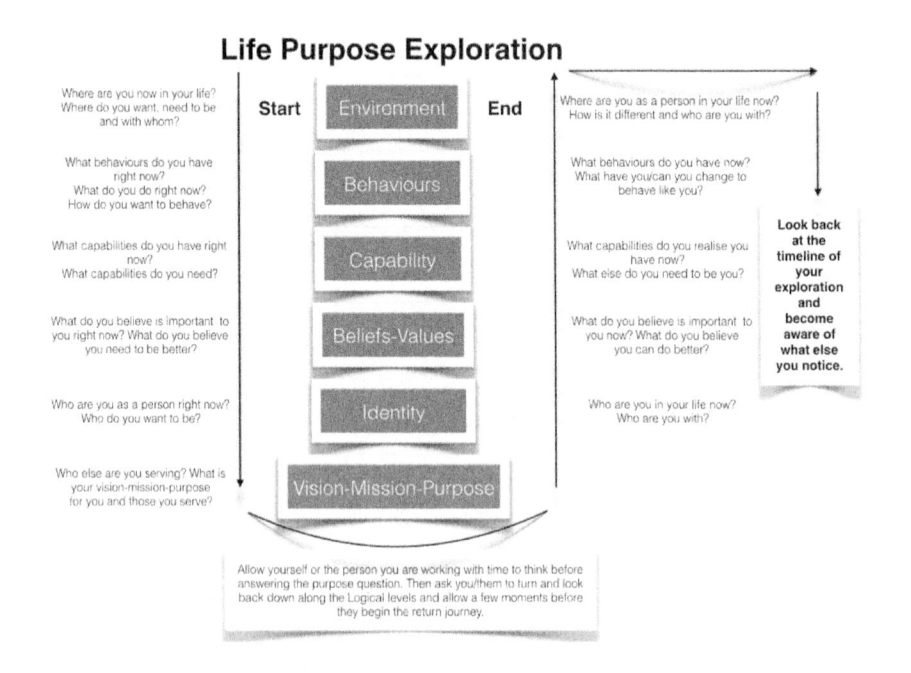

Life Purpose Exploration

Start side	Level	End side
Where are you now in your life? Where do you want, need to be and with whom?	Environment	Where are you as a person in your life now? How is it different and who are you with?
What behaviours do you have right now? What do you do right now? How do you want to behave?	Behaviours	What behaviours do you have now? What have you/can you change to behave like you?
What capabilities do you have right now? What capabilities do you need?	Capability	What capabilities do you realise you have now? What else do you need to be you?
What do you believe is important to you right now? What do you believe you need to be better?	Beliefs-Values	What do you believe is important to you now? What do you believe you can do better?
Who are you as a person right now? Who do you want to be?	Identity	Who are you in your life now? Who are you with?
Who else are you serving? What is your vision-mission-purpose for you and those you serve?	Vision-Mission-Purpose	

Look back at the timeline of your exploration and become aware of what else you notice.

Allow yourself or the person you are working with time to think before answering the purpose question. Then ask you/them to turn and look back down along the Logical levels and allow a few moments before they begin the return journey.

THE BEHAVIOURAL CHANGE LEARNING CYCLE

There is nothing permanent except change. Change is the only constant. Change alone is unchanging." Heraclitus

Social and Psychological Sciences has seen a coming together of eastern (philosophy) and western (rational) thinking. New discoveries in Neuroscience have also greatly contributed to our understanding of coaching and the nature of change.

This Behavioural Change Learning Cycle is a blend of two older models:

> 3.1 The Behavioural Change Cycle - Proch Clemente
> https://en.wikipedia.org/wiki/Transtheore
> 3.2 The Fours Stages of Learning - Martin
> https://en.wikipedia.org/wiki/Four_stages

It occurred to me a few years ago that there was a direct correlation between the two and as I looked into this in more detail, it became clear to me that as I over-layed the two models, they seamlessly integrated in explaining in more depth, how we learn to change our behaviours.

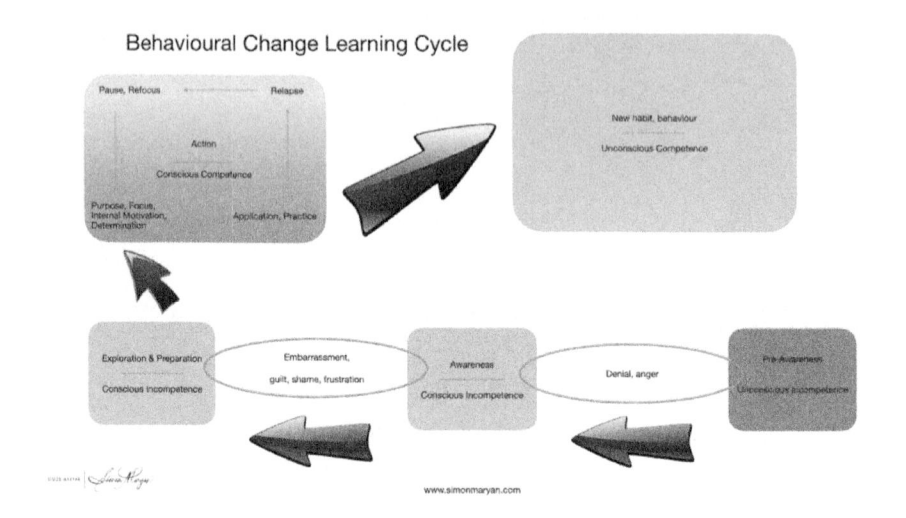

Four Stages of learning Behavioral Change Learning Cycle

Four Stages of learning Behavioural Change Learning Cycle

Stage	Learning Cycle	Behavioural Change
1	Unconscious Incompetence	Pre-Awareness
	(informed by others - denial & anger) individual is not yet ready to acknowledge that their behaviour needs to be changed.	
2	Conscious Incompetence	Awareness
	(embarrassment, guilt, shame, frustration) individual acknowledges the negative consequences of their existing behaviour - but is not ready or sure it is time for a change.	
2	Conscious Incompetence	Exploration
	(exploring possibilities and options for learning required skills and behaviours, external assistance)	
3	Conscious Competence	Purpose & Focus

- Purpose & focus
- Internal Motivation
- Determination
- Application-Practice
- Relapse-Pause-Refocus

Feedback loop where the determinations developed from internal motivation, which gives focus on purpose which drives internal motivation and so on.

Application of practice of the new skills/behaviours is the action and this takes conscious effort to apply as it is new. When too much is happening or stress leads to an emotional overload and overwhelm then the old habit/behaviour kicks in causing relapse.

As a relapse occurs it is time to pause, refocus on the desired new skill/habit/behaviour, reconnect with purpose and focus on the internal motivation to reignite the determination to continue applying the daily practice. Overtime, awareness of signs of an impending relapse become clearer and more obvious and this develops the ability to take proactive action

| 4 | Unconscious Competence | New Habit/Behaviour |

The new habit/behaviour is now second nature and has superseded the old default, negative behaviour. The new behaviour is acted out without conscious thought, leading to what Prochaska and Di Clemente referred to as Transcendence.

| 4 | Unconscious Competence | Transendence |

Permanent place. For example, a person's old habits no longer feel a part of their life, they do not fir who they are now or who they want to become. To return to their old habits would feel foreign and strange, uncomfortable.

Change is an enigma and yet sustained, desirable change (SDC) drives adaptation, growth and life itself. In this book we continuously attempt to answer four fundamental questions:

1. What is the process of achieving sustained, desirable change?
2. What is our role in helping create change?
3. Why the real self is fundamental to
4. Intentional change?
5. Why are emotions the key to successful change?

THE INTENTIONAL CHANGE MODEL

In a research study, a group of researchers from Case Western Reserve University made several discoveries about when coaching is not effective. This followed 17 years of longitudinal studies showing adults can change their habits and develop competencies (both cognitive and emotional intelligence competencies). **When adults change their behaviour, they follow a series of epiphanies, or discoveries that has been called the Intentional Change Model.**

In Purposeful Intentional Change - the ideal self is the emotional driver of intentional change. **The components of a person's personal vision come from their ideal self.**

Intentional change is hard work and often fails because of lack of sufficient drive and the proper intrinsic motivation for it. The below model of the ideal self creates a comprehensive context within which a person (or a group) can formulate why they want to adapt, evolve, or maintain their current desired state.

Intentional change theory (ICT) is a complex adaptive system. Based on theories of individual self-directed learning (Boyatzis, 1999, 2001), **ICT involves a sequence of five discontinuous and iterative discoveries:**

1. The ideal self or personal vision
2. The real self and its comparison to the ideal self resulting in an assessment of one's strengths and weaknesses
3. A learning agenda and plan
4. Experimentation and practice with the new behaviour, thoughts, feelings, or perceptions
5. Resonant relationships that enable a person to experience and process each discovery in the process

These below discoveries occur at the above listed 5 levels.

1. **For instance, in the first discovery, an individual might engage in various processes seeking a personal vision or definition of the ideal self – a realistic image of a desired future.** This image is based on positive attributes of hope, selfefficacy, and optimism, and is founded upon a person's core identity and enduring strengths. The Ideal self is the personality we would like to be. It consists of our goals and ambitions, and is dynamic in nature. Our ideal self is forever

changing. The ideal self of our childhood is not the same as the ideal self of our late teens etc. There is no way to tell what people think of us. What we know is who we are and what we want to be. As individuals we create these two domains, the "Real self" (who we are) and the "Ideal self" (what we want to be).

The ideal self is a primary source of positive affect and psychophysiological arousal helping provide the drive for intentional change. Most coaching frameworks or change theories examine only portions of this model and, therefore, leave major components unaddressed. The ideal self is composed of three major components: - an image of a desired future; -hope (and its constituents, self-efficacy and optimism); and -a comprehensive sense of one's core identity (past strengths, traits, and other enduring dispositions).

The real self is everything we have become. All our actions and beliefs are inside the real self domain. This is what people see you as and how they perceive you. The ideal self is what we aim to become. This domain is an intimate one and is not seen by others. For example, your ideal self wants to be a good person, so you behave by doing things that are aligned with that view. Such behaviours may include helping others or donating goods. The point is that you are acting in a way that you want to be seen. Your ideal self (being good) is congruent with your real self (acting like a good person).

These two domains overlap; it brings pleasure and peace of mind to you.

When the first discovery does not occur, people don't change. That is the reason most people think leaders are born not made. Despite the efforts of well-intentioned, sensitive, thoughtful people, most education and training does not produce sustainable changes in behaviour. To explore why this occurs, take a moment to complete the reflective exercise below.

SOLO EXERCISE:

Self - Who helped Me and Who Tried' Reflective Exercise:

- Think about the people in your life who have helped you the most. Think of those who helped you to achieve what you have in life and at work and to become the person you are. Write their names on a sheet of paper. Next to each name, describe moments you remember with them that had a lasting impact on you. What did they say or do? Thinking back about those instances, what did you learn or take away from them?

- Now, think of the people who have tried to help, manage or coach you in the past two years. Think of the moments you've had with them. What did they say or do?

- Go back to each of the moments remembered in the first list and ask yourself what stage of the Intentional change model was involved.

When a person does this exercise, they have warm, emotional reactions to the memories of the people who helped them. The feelings come back strongly as they remember moments that may have been tender or challenging, but had a lasting impact. When Case university recorded these reflections and coded them for which aspect of the change process was primarily involved, they discovered that 80% of the moments people recalled someone helping them extend their dreams, reach for new aspirations, consider what it means to be successful or a good person. In other words, these people help us recreate a new Ideal Self (i.e., Personal Vision) or endorse our Strengths and capability in a way we doubted or never considered.

2. **An individual at the second discovery may explore the real self particularly in comparison with the ideal self; that is,** explicitly how does it vary from the ideal self – what are the strengths and gaps. 360 degree feedback tools can be used to provide objective assessments.

If the person feels sufficiently motivated to change they will "take a look in the mirror" to get a better sense of who they are. This enables them to discover the strengths that they can build on and the gaps that exist between their current real and ideal selves.

Note: -if you want to know what people think of you, just ask yourself, "Am I the person who I think I am?"

3. The focus of the learning agenda or plan is to operationalise the vision including establishment of goals, action plans, and measurement tools. This is a critical step as the vision is now being shared more broadly with others and possibly within a stakeholder field.
4. Plans should anticipate experiments and innovations that will be realised in the fourth discovery – freedom of the individual to experiment and practice with the new behaviours and skill sets. Experiments and innovative practices will be more effective if employed in safe and encouraging atmospheres because there is relatively less risk or consequences of individual failure
5. **The last individual discovery – developing resonant relationships** – means surrounding oneself with trusting supporters of the desired change.

At some point in the process we discover that it is much easier to change ourselves with the support of a coach and others we can trust. Indeed, it may not be possible to achieve that change without the encouragement of other people who are welldisposed towards us. In order to change we need to take risks. We discover that to feel able to experiment and practice we need to feel a measure of psychological safety. We can find that in supportive and trusting relationships.

The fifth discovery could be the first. It is about establishing a trusting relationship with someone who can help you through each step. This is where the coach of today becomes an essential element in the growth process by helping people capture and become their dreams -realise their vision.

Summary: The Ideal Self manifests as a personal vision of what a person hopes to achieve in their life and work, or as an image of the kind of person they want to be.

So, to help our clients change, one of the most powerful things we can help them do is activate the force of their Ideal Self.

Boyatzis & Akrivou in "The ideal self as a driver of change" (*Journal of Management Development. 2006, 25(7), 624-642.*) propose that there are three elements to developing a healthy and robust Ideal Self that a professional coach can help someone with:

1. **Awareness**: Articulating and making explicit their Ideal Self by increasing their mindfulness of it and its components (see diagram previous page).

2. **Importance**: Raising the importance of their Ideal Self by increasing the intensity of their desire for the components of their Ideal Self.
3. **Coherence**: Integrating all the components of the Ideal Self with the their desired life and future.

Note: The Ideal Self is different from the "Ought Self", which is someone else's version of what your Ideal Self should be, which you have mistaken for your Ideal Self. The Ought Self can masquerade as a very convincing Ideal Self - as coaches we need to be alert to this and help unmask the impostor! (in the nicest possible way of course).

ANCHORING

An **anchor** is a stimulus that creates a response in either you or in another person. When an individual is at the peak of an experience, during an intense, emotional state, and if a specific stimulus is applied, a neurological link is established between the emotional state and the stimulus. It is always fully associated. Anchoring can occur naturally or be set up intentionally and can assist in gaining access to past states and linking the past state to the present and the future.

In 1902, **Dr. Edwin B. Twitmyer** submitted a paper to the American Medical Association called "Stimulus Response". It outlined the hammer-to-knee-reflex. The American Medical

Association was not very interested. In 1904, **Ivan P. Pavlov**, a Russian, read Dr. Twitmyer's paper. In 1936, after years of research with dogs, he submitted a paper to the Russian Medical Society called "Conditioned Reflexes", and he got the credit for discovering stimulus-response. In his research, he anchored the sound of a tuning fork to when the dogs were hungry and would salivate. Anchoring is fundamentally the process of stimulusresponse.

There are many kinds of anchors. Some are useful and some are not. Here are a few examples:

Alarm clock
Advertising jingles
Someone touching you
Old songs
Tastes and smells
Traffic lights
Faces
Voices
Buildings and places
Applause
Activities
Holding hands

Many behavioural psychologists believe we operate our lives totally with conditioned reflexes. Many also believe that learning is setting up new anchors and responding to them.

Under certain circumstances an anchor will last forever, particularly if the experience was highly emotionally-charged. It is really useful to be able to anchor a state in any person at any time in any modality.

USES OF ANCHORING

Anchoring has numerous uses. The reason why they are so useful can be summarised by probably the only equation in NLP:

PRESENT STATE + RESOURCES = DESIRED STATE

'Resources' in Neuro Linguistic terms are the personal attributes we have or would like to have, such as:

- confidence
- motivated
- energised
- calm

By gaining access to these types of resources, we can help ourselves and turn seemingly challenging situations into situations with possibilities. The process we use is 'Anchoring'.

It is difficult to imagine a situation when feeling at your best, in a resourceful state, would not be useful.

- To feel at your best whenever you want to
- To help other feels at their best whenever they want to (coaching)
- Interviews
- Exams
- First dates
- Doing sport
- Making presentations

FIVE KEYS TO ANCHORING

I TURN

This mnemonic was created by Advanced Neuro Dynamics

1. **I** — INTENSITY of the experience.
   An anchor should be applied when the client is fully associated in an intense state. The more intense the experience, the better the anchor will stick. You use your sensory acuity and calibration skills to notice when the client is going into a specific state.

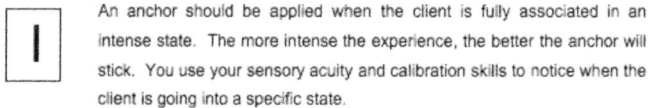

2. **T** — TIMING of the anchor.
   When you see the beginning of the state, apply the anchor. When you see the state reach its peak, let it go. This can vary typically from five to fifteen seconds. (See "Application of an Anchor.") This is the basis of **precision anchoring**.

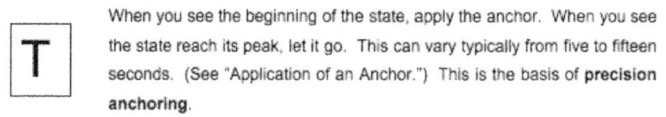

3. **U** — UNIQUENESS of the stimulus.
   A handshake, although it is an anchor, may be too common. The anchor must be in a unique location that will not be accidentally or inadvertently touched.

4. **R** — REPLICABILITY of the stimulus.
   The anchor has to be replicable in the relevant situations.

5. **N** — NUMBER of times.
   Repetition of the stimulus, the number of times the stimulus is applied. If you keep adding, or stacking, anchors, it becomes even more powerful. The more often, the more powerful will be the anchor.

THE ANCHORING PROCESS

Here are the basic steps to anchoring. The details will depend on whether you are asking someone to anchor themselves, or whether you are anchoring them.

1. **Pre-frame:** Build rapport with the person. Get permission to touch if relevant (hands, shoulders, head) Explain anchor (in this context) is set by touching index finger and thumb together on hand of choice.

2. **Immersion/Recall** — Have the person immerse themselves in the relaxed state of mind and body they have self induced through the Whole Brain State exercise, and if this is a follow on session ask them to recall vividly the experience. The best states to anchor are those that occur naturally and that are vivid and highly associated.

Can you remember the last time when you were totally <u>calm and relaxed.</u> Can you remember in every sense?

Many people remember a number of experiences. Get the client to remember one specific time.

As you go back to that time now (pause), go right back to that time and see what you're seeing, hear what you're hearing, and really feel the feelings, as you feel totally <u>calm and relaxed</u>.

NB: For best effect be in that state yourself

3. Associate - Make sure the client fully (re)associates into the state.

exhalations to reach the optimum inflation/peak experience.

4. **Pause after each peak state** - At the end of each exhalation/peak state, release index finger and thumb and allow a few normal breaths before repeating the process for a total of five times.

5. **Repeat** - Repeat steps 3, 4 & 5 five times or as many as necessary.

6. **Test** - Test three times - Past, Future & Present. Test the anchor by asking them to think of a time in the past that was stressful, overwhelming and where it would have been useful to have been able to intervene on themselves. Ask them to remember it as if it is happening NOW and to see, hear and feel everything that is going on, and at the point that they want to apply their anchor, just touch their index finger and thumb together and notice how it changes what happens. Watch their response and ask what is happening and how is it different?

Repeat for a future situation and how they imagine it will unfold based on previous experience. Watch their response and ask what is happening and how is it different?

Finally test in the present by asking them how they feel and then to touch their index finger and thumb together and notice what happens. Watch their response and ask what is happening and how is it different?

The Immediate Care Process

THE ANCHORING PROCESS VISUAL GUIDE

Icarus Anchoring Process

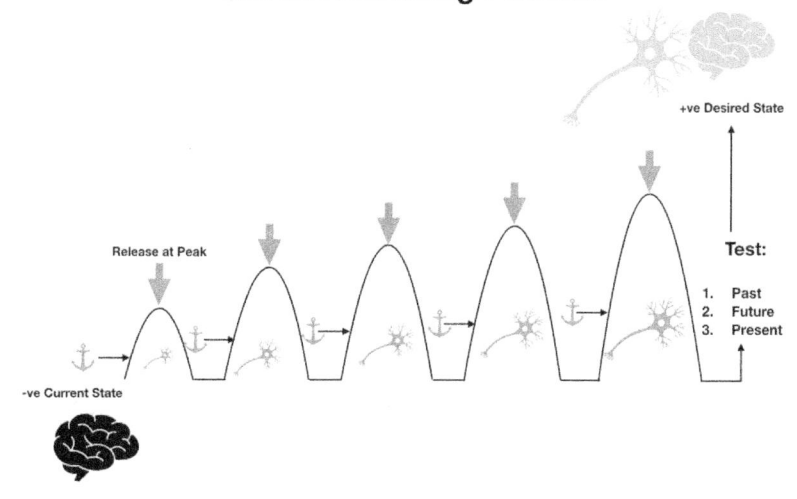

Release at Peak

+ve Desired State

Test:
1. Past
2. Future
3. Present

-ve Current State

PART 2
PSYCHOLOGICAL SKILLS

NEGATIVE THOUGHT PATTERN INTERRUPT

This is an extremely simple and highly effective exercise to apply with yourself or someone else in the midst of a mental health crisis for whatever reason.

When we become overloaded and over-whelmed we feel stressed, we become anxious and panicky, our thoughts tend to focus on the negative and play the 'What if' game. We can become consumed with black and white, catastrophic thinking that feeds the vicious cycle we have spun into. This type of thought pattern is highly destructive and leads to self-sabotage by perpetuating the downward, negative spiral into the fog of panic attacks as we lose our clarity of mind and thought. We lose our sense of purpose, our sense of self and loose direction and our focus the multitude of negative thoughts in the vortex that has consumed our mind.

This exercise is a simple, quick and effective method of interrupting the thought pattern and disconnecting the feelings associated with those thoughts. It utilises many of the principles in Part 1 such as the following:

- Pre-framing, de-framing, re-framing

- Outcomes and ecology
- Cause and effect
- Communication model
- Sensory acuity - observation and utilisation
- Rapport
- Representational systems and language
- Verbal anchoring

This exercise has been adapted from the original work of Stephen Brooks who is a world leading teacher of Ericksonian Hypnosis and Psychotherapy. It was refined initially to treat veterans struggling with PTSD and the collective of symptoms associated with it, as in its original form it did not fit with the military mindset. Veterans are a tough audience in that respect and are generally brutally honest in their feedback and shut down when they do not like or agree with the process.

The refinement has lead to this simplistic approach on the surface with much going on at many different levels for the client, which is why this has such a significant impact in such a short space of time. The process is outlined below.

THE PROCESS

1. **Build Rapport** - talk calmly and rationally, ask person questions about themselves: ask their name (if you don't know), what they do etc. Ask what's going on, draw information out of them gently. Ask them if they'd like you to help them.
2. **Pre-frame** - talk about negative mind games, thoughts and feelings. Explain that you can help them counter the negative thoughts and feelings with a simple positive mind game that stops the thoughts and removes the feelings. Ask them if they would like you to help them do that.
3. **Explain the game** -
    - they are to acknowledge the thoughts and not pay attention to them
    - focus on the feelings associated with the thoughts
    - repeat a short sentence out loud over and over on a loop while focusing on the feelings until they intuitively stop
    - the sentence is "It's just a thought"

- when they stop ask them to try to identify why they stopped
- find thoughts again and assess associated feelings now compared to at the start on a 1-10 scale

4. **Repeat** - repeat this process for as many cycles as is required to reduce intensity of feelings to a level they are comfortable with, or completely gone.

THE DETAIL

As stated earlier the process is simple on the surface with so much going on at many different levels, and in this section we explain the mechanics behind the process.

1. **Build Rapport** - *talk calmly and rationally, ask person questions about themselves: ask their name (if you don't know), what they do etc. Ask what's going on, draw information out of them gently. Ask them if they'd like you to help them.*

Stage 1. This is the crucial first step and if rapport is not reached then the entire process will not happen. At the point of crisis the person is fully engaged with their Limbic System and emotionally driven, they are not generally able to think rationally themselves and as such they need help to create that shift in perception and begin to engage their rational mind. Asking them simple questions about themselves will begin to interrupt their current thought pattern, and asking what is going on enables the person to start to process in a different way. Holding those thoughts

in and not expressing them perpetuates the negative cycle, verbalising allows a shift in perception and processing.

2. **Pre-frame, Re-frame and De-frame**— *talk about negative mind games, thoughts and feelings. Explain that you can help them counter the negative thoughts and feelings with a simple positive mind game that stops the thoughts and removes the feelings. Ask them if they would like you to help them do that.*

Stage 2. This begins to shift perception by creating choice when there was only one perceived option available due to the self limiting mindset (at Effect) created through the overload and overwhelm. This can also create confusion at first as the person may draw a blank, this is good because whenever there is a blank there is something behind it that they have unconsciously blocked for some reason. Changing their frame of reference by re-framing and de-framing opens up possibilities that they hadn't been aware of until that point. Once a person is aware of new options, both consciously and unconsciously, they can not look at their perceived problem in the same way and change is then inevitable.

3. Explain the game -

- *they are to acknowledge the thoughts and not pay direct attention to them -* **dissociation, disconnect**

- *focus on the feelings associated with the thoughts* - **change focus of attention, disconnect**
- *repeat a short sentence out loud over and over on a loop while focusing on the feelings until they intuitively stop* - **dissociation, distraction and interrupt**
- *the sentence is "It's just a thought"* - **dissociation, distraction, confusion and interrupt**
- *when they stop ask them to try to identify why they stopped* - **re-process**
- *find thoughts again and assess associated feelings now compared to at the start on a 1-10 scale* - **re-process**

4. **Repeat** - repeat this process for as many cycles as is required to reduce intensity of feelings to a level they are comfortable with, or completely gone. **Reinforce positive effect and diffuse previous state**

WHOLE BRAIN STATE AND ANCHOR

In positive psychology, **Flow State**, also known colloquially as being in **the Z** of operation in which a person performing an activity is fully immersed in a feeling of energised focus, full involvement, and enjoyment in the process of the activity. In essence, flow is characterised by complete absorption in what one does, and a resulting loss in one's sense of space and time.

Named by Mihály Csíkszentmihályi in 1975, the concept has been widely referred to across a variety of fields (and has an especially big recognition in occupational therapy), though the concept has existed for thousands of years under other names, notably in some Eastern religions.

Flow shares many characteristics with hyperfocus. However, hyper-focus is not always described in a positive light. Some examples include spending "too much" time playing video games or getting side-tracked and pleasurably absorbed by one aspect of an assignment or task to the detriment of the overall assignment. In some cases, hyper-focus can "capture" a person, perhaps causing them to appear unfocused or to start several projects, but complete few.

We utilise hyper-focus by creating a whole brain state that draws someones focus internally and allowing external stimulus to become irrelevant, thereby reducing stress by filtering out external stimulus.

Components

Jeanne Nakamura and Csíkszentmihály identify the following six factors as encompassing an experience of flow:

1. Intense and focused concentration on the present moment
2. Merging of action and awareness
3. A loss of reflective self-consciousness
4. A sense of personal control or agency over the situation or activity
5. A distortion of temporal experience, one's subjective experience of time is altered
6. Experience of the activity as intrinsically rewarding, also referred to as autotelic experience

Those aspects can appear independently of each other, but only in combination do they constitute a so-called *flow experience*. Additionally, psychology writer Kendra Cherry has mentioned three other components that

Csíkszentmihályi lists as being a part of the flow experience:

1. "Immediate feedback"
2. Feeling that you have the potential to succeed
3. Feeling so engrossed in the experience, that other needs become negligible

Just as with the conditions listed above, these conditions can be independent of one another.

In any given moment, there is a great deal of information made available to each individual. Psychologists have found that one's mind can attend to only a certain amount of information at a time. According to Csikszentmihályi's 2004 TED talk, that number is about "110 bits of information per second". That may seem like a lot of information, but simple daily tasks take quite a lot of information. Just decoding speech takes about 60 bits of information per second. That is why when having a conversation one cannot focus as much attention on other things.

For the most part (except for basic bodily feelings like hunger and pain, which are innate), people are able to decide what they want to focus their attention on. However, when one is in the flow state, they are completely engrossed with the one task at hand and, without making the conscious decision to do so, loose awareness of all other things: time, people, distractions, and even basic bodily needs. This occurs because all of the attention of the person in the whole brain state is on the task at hand; there is no more attention to be allocated.

The whole state has been described as the "optimal experience" in that one gets to a level of high gratification, relaxation and hyperfocus and awareness from the experience. Achieving this experience is considered to be personal and "depends on the ability" of the individual. One's capacity and desire to overcome challenges in order to achieve their ultimate goals not only leads to the optimal experience, but also to a sense of life satisfaction overall. Our initial goal with veterans is to enable them to feel a sense of control over their mind, thoughts and feelings again, this boosts their confidence and self belief that they can improve and get better.

This sense of life satisfaction is very much the purpose and intention of this next exercise, so again we will explain, demonstrate, take questions then you will practice individually and then work in pairs.

THE PROCESS

This exercise is in two parts, both parts can be lead by a practitioner or can be self lead after having been guided through the routine just once and the process is as follows:

PART 1: WHOLE BRAIN STATE

- sit comfortably in a chair with legs uncrossed and feet flat on the floor and forearms supported on the arm of a chair, or lay down on the floor or a bed.
- breathe in through the nose to a count of three while in your head say the word 'Relax, Relax, Relax,' at the same time close your eyes and lift your forearm as if breathing your hand up to your nose. Upper arm does not move and elbow remains in contact with the supporting surface.
- hold breath for a count of three.
- breathe out for a count of three, lower forearm and hand down to rest on the supporting surface, as if

blowing it back down and allow your eyes to open as you relax even deeper with your eyes open. This step is like a sigh of relief as you let go of tension and stress with each breathe out.

- hold breath for a count of three
- repeat this on a continuous, fluid loop until the following happens: either eyes stay open or stay closed, arm doesn't lift because it feels too heavy to lift, or it stays floating in the air somewhere.
- Whatever happens just let it happen.
- you may feel slightly woozy, light headed and floaty, this is perfectly normal and is a clear indicator that you are accessing your Whole Brain State
- You may feel resistance in your mind to the sensation of relaxing. This is very common as the brain is so accustomed to being in high alert and it resists out of habit with a misplaced safety measure. Allow the resistance to burn itself out while focusing on the breathing, lifting and lowering.
- It is normal for the pattern to go out of sink, this is good as it is another sign that the brain is lowing down, relaxing and operating at a different frequency

PART 2: ANCHOR

- Use the Icarus Anchor to link this Whole Brain State to a simple physical action - touch index finger and thumb
- Get permission to touch if relevant/appropriate/possible (hands, shoulders, head)
- **Revivify** — utilise the Whole Brain State
- **NB** Get into the state yourself
- Associate - Make sure the client is fully associated into the state
- to release at the peak of the experience. Touch index finger and thumb together
- **Repeat** - over 5 breaths
- **Test** - Test the anchor with a past then a future scenario. Distract and finally test present. Person should feel increased relaxation even though they already feel relaxed.

EYE PATTERNING AND REIMPRINTING

This requires the use of **Pacing** and **Leading** and specific use of **Eye Accessing Cue**s along with identifying and utilising the persons predicates and changing the sub modality sequencing of the problem memory, behaviour, thought pattern etc. This blend of skills enables the Practitioner to move someone through different representational systems while directing the

Eye Patterning piece where the aim is to direct an individual to follow the movements you suggest, and enable them to reframe, reprocess and re-integrate through the re-imprinting. In this way you can lead a person into different (more comfortable) body postures, and also to be able to lead them into more positive thought patterns and beliefs and open them up to new perceptions of their past, present and future.

The eye patterning is used to reframe the memory of a negative situation that has been imprinted in the mind of the person. When we are anxious, nervous, scared etc we have a tendency to look down and see everything in our minds eye down low, where as when we remember a positive memory that has been imprinted we tend to look forwards and upwards. We can take advantage of these natural tendencies, along with the other accessing cues to change the perception of the event and re-imprint a new frame and perception.

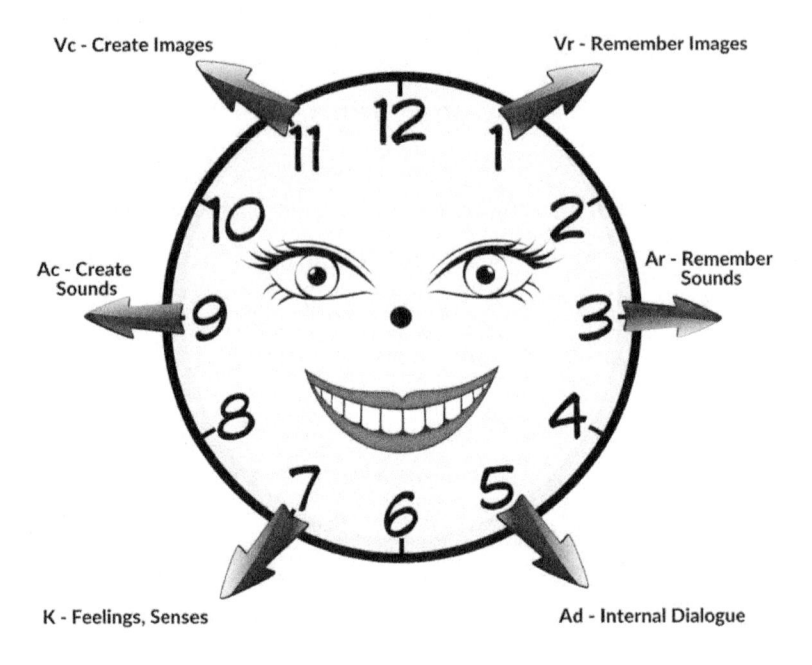

Vc - Create Images
Vr - Remember Images
Ac - Create Sounds
Ar - Remember Sounds
K - Feelings, Senses
Ad - Internal Dialogue

WHAT ARE IMPRINTS & HOW ARE THEY CREATED

An imprint is a significant event from the past that is encoded in a specific format containing sensory information, facts and beliefs or cluster of beliefs about that event. Every form of healing, both physical and psychological acknowledges the fact that present behaviours are often created by past behaviours and past events. What's important to us about past experiences is not the content of what happened, but the impression it left and the beliefs formed by a person as a result of how they processed the event at the time.

The early understanding of imprinting comes from the work of Konrad Lorenz who studied the behaviour of ducklings after they hatch. He discovered that the ducklings would imprint a mother figure in the first day or so of life. They did that by sorting for movement, so that if something moved just after they hatched, they would follow it and "it" became their mother. Lorenz would move and the ducklings would follow. He found that if he reintroduced them to their real mother later on they would ignore her and continue following him. In the mornings he would go outside and find the ducklings curled up around his boots instead of in their own nest.

Lorenz once reported that a ping pong ball rolled by one of the eggs as it hatched and the emerging duckling imprinted to the ping pong ball making it its "mother'. later in life the duck would shun others of its kind at mating season and try to mate with other round objects instead.

Konrad Lorenz and his colleagues believed that imprints were established at certain neurologically critical periods and that once the critical period had passed, whatever had been imprinted was permanent and not subject to change.

Timothy Leary investigated the imprint phenomenon in human beings. He contended that the human nervous system was more sophisticated than that of ducklings and other animals. He established that under the right conditions, content that had been imprinted at earlier critical periods could be accessed and reprogrammed or re-imprinted.

Leary also identified several significant developmental critical periods in human beings. Imprints established during these periods generated core beliefs that shaped the personality and intelligence of the individual. The primary critical periods involved the establishment of imprints determining beliefs about biological survival, emotional attachments and well-being, intellectual dexterity, social role, aesthetic appreciation and metacognition, or the awareness of one's own thought processes. This meant that health problems might stem back to core beliefs and supporting behaviours established during the critical biological survival period, while phobias could have their roots in the emotional well-being period. Learning handicaps might derive from imprints formed during the critical period involving intellectual dexterity, and so on.

Robert Dilts developments of the Neuro Linguistic Re-Imprinting process grew out of a series of seminars he conducted with Leary. It was as a result of his work with Leary that he realised that some traumatic episodes experienced by people were more than just bad memories that could be dealt with by using simple integration techniques. They were often belief and identity forming imprints that formed the cornerstones of a persons personality, and therefore required a different approach in order to influence the person in an appropriate and lasting way.

Imprints can be significant "positive" experiences that lead to useful beliefs, and they can be traumatic or problematic experiences that lead to limiting belief sets. Typically, but not always, they involve the unconscious modelling of significant others.

Compare the duck's behaviour with human behaviour using child abuse as a point of comparison. Research validates that often people who have been abused as children unconsciously get into relationships, as adults, that repeat their childhood experience. For example, often women who have been abused as children marry menthe abuse them as adults. Males who're beaten as a child may abuse their own children. If they were beaten by their mothers, they may get into relationships where they are somehow the lesser person. Research shows that women who were beaten by their mothers are apt to be more violent with their own children than those who weren't . Imprints are one explanation of this phenomenon. People abused as children can imprint that this is typical behaviour associated with fathers, mothers, husbands or wives.

At the time the ducklings were hatching, they didn't think "That's a weird looking mother, I'd better check it out." Their brains were probably saying something like, "This is how mothers are." Human beings do the same sort of thing, yet we have the ability to re-imprint.

MODELLING OTHERS PERSPECTIVES

An imprint isn't necessarily logical, it's something that's intuitive and it typically happens at a critical developmental period. In childhood, most of us don't have a real sense of self-identity, so we pretend we're somebody else and we often take on the role model, lock, stock and barrel. We can end up like the ducklings that did not question who their mother was.

Who you are as an adult, is in many ways, an incorporation of the adult models you grew up with. Your model of being an adult has the features of the past significant role models in your life. Features that have been stuck in early ways of believing and behaving that you made a part of you at an early age. These beliefs and behaviours emerge when you reach a certain age and are no longer a child. This is why it's as important to deal with the other people involved as well as the younger self in the reimprinting process.

IDENTIFYING AND WORKING WITH IMPRINTS

The hardest part of changing the belief system for an imprint is the fact that the belief is likely to be out of conscious awareness. The most significant behaviours are usually the ones that are the most habitual, and these are the behaviours that people are the least aware of. When using an anchored feeling as a guide to past memories, the experiences remembered first may not may not be as important as going back to the point where the person feels confused and says "I didn't know I did that." This is a significant discovery and is often seen as a sticking point. However it is at this point that we know the person has reached the right point in terms of identifying the circumstances at which they created the limiting belief.

BRICK WALLS & FEELING STUCK

Sometimes when working with an anchored feeling, even an intense one, and hold it to assist the person in remembering past experiences, the person hits a brick wall. Suddenly there's nothing to work with, this is because some people learn to dissociate themselves from the pain to avoid what might be coming. At this point the brick wall or dissociated state can be anchored and taken back in time to search for a significant past imprint. Patience is required here as the person finds pieces of the puzzle, often in the form of still images in their minds eye as the put the jigsaw back together recreating the imprint situation.

Alternatively, when a person feels stuck, immediately interrupt them and anchor them to a resourceful state they have experienced before, such as courage or power; a generic resource that would be useful in many different situations. Then take the resource anchor back into the sticking point to help the person move beyond it.

Often therapeutic stories (metaphors) are useful when working toward integration. When a sticking point is discovered where the conscious mind is doing one thing and the unconscious another, it's useful to use a metaphor, particularly if the person is saying something like "It just doesn't make sense."

Einstein has a great quote that says "Everything should be made as simple as possible, but not simpler." This can be a useful metaphor for people who are stuck and suggest that if they try too hard to make something happen faster or less simply, then they will get stuck and meet some form of resistance. The great thing about metaphors is that they are processed by both brain hemispheres, so they bridge thinking gaps. Even if the metaphor is doing nothing more that repeating what you just said by restating it in an analogy or story, it is still being understood at a different level.

So in summary, an imprint experience generally involves the unconscious role modelling of a significant person or people from a persons past. The purpose of re-imprinting is to give new choices in the way a person thinks about the old imprint experience. These choices assist in changing beliefs they had made about themselves, the world and the other people involved.

To accomplish the Re-imprinting you need to add the resources they would have needed at the time of the experience in order to have more choices about their behaviour. They will also need to add resources for the other people involved in those earlier experiences.

EYE PATTERNING AND REIMPRINTING PROCESS

This is an adaptation of Robert Dilts Re-Imprinting Process from his book "Beliefs - Pathways to Health and Well-Being."

Robert Dilts, Tim Halbom and Suzi Smith 2012; p.87; Crown House Publishing

1. Ask the person to visualise the problem and notice where they look e.g. up to their left to remember initially and then generally for a problem memory down towards the floor or straight in front. Ask them to tell you where they see the memory.

2. Ask the person to look down and to the right to access the feelings associated with the memory, then to look horizontally to the left to remember the sounds associated with the memory, then when they've done that look up to their left to access the images associated with the memory. Draw out the key sub-modalities associated with the memory. When they have accessed all this information ask them to move the memory to where it feels more comfortable to view it.

3. Anchor it. **NOTE:** Most people want to avoid these feelings because they are uncomfortable. However, it is important to remember that avoiding them will not resolve the limitation. Have the person stay with the feeling and remember back to the earliest experience of the feeling associated with the sticking point. While the person is in that associated, regressed state, ask them to verbalise the generalisations and/or beliefs that were formed from that experience.

4. Ask the person to look up and move the image, sounds and feelings upwards and to their right so that it is in edit mode. This is because typically up to the left is remembered and up to the right is creating. Now ask them to dissociate themselves from it so it and they are no longer in it, so that they can see themselves in the image. Ask them to verbalise the sub-modalities associated with the image any other generalisations and/or beliefs that were formed as a result of the imprint experience. Beliefs are often formed "after the fact."

5. Ask them to look down and to the right to find the positive intent or secondary gain for the feeling of sticking point and when they find them to look at the dissociated image. Also if there were others involved in the memory, find the positive intent of their behaviour as well, if they want to. This may

be done by directly asking the people in the image. Get the person to check for feelings down to the right, sounds middle left and images upper left. If they can't find them get them to create them by looking middle right for sounds and upper right for images. Once complete take these elements and look again at the dissociated image.

6. Identify and anchor the resources or choices that the person and the important others each individually needed then, and did not have then, but the person does have now. Remember the person does not have to limit themselves to the capabilities they or the important others had then, just as long as the person, not the important others, has the resources available to them now in order that they can use them to help change that experience. Get the person to check for

7. feelings down to the right, sounds middle left and images upper left. If they can't find them get them to create the ones they need by looking middle right for sounds and upper right for images.

8. For each important other person involved in the imprint memory/experience, have the person replay the movie of the experience, seeing how different it would be if the necessary resources had been available to that person. Do this one at a time for each person making sure the identified resources would be sufficient to change the

The Immediate Care Process

experience. If not go back to steps 4 and 5 and identify other positive intentions or resources that may have been overlooked. Get the person to check for feelings down to the right, sounds middle left and images upper left. If they can't find them get them to create them by looking middle right for sounds and upper right for images. After the resources have been added, ask the person to verbalise what new generalisations and/or beliefs they would choose as a result of adding these new resources.

9. Utilising the resources in step 5, have the person relive the imprint experience from the new point of view. Have them actually associate, and imagine stepping into it and see the experience from this new perspective. Next have them finish by stepping into the younger version of themselves and reexperience it as their younger self. Go through the new experience enough times that it is as strong as the original imprint. Ask the person to update or modify the generalisations and/or beliefs they would now make about the experience.

10. Have the person come back through time from the point of the original imprint to the present. Suggest that as they come back up through time, they can think of other occasions in their life when these resources that are anchored

in now would also have been a useful addition in changing other experiences. Get the person to check for feelings down to the right, sounds middle left and images upper left for a confirmation check that they have made the changes they needed to make.

11. Ask the person if there are any other changes they feel they want or need to make in order to be comfortable with this new memory. Again Get the person to check for feelings down to the right, sounds middle left and images upper left. If they can't find them get them to create them by looking middle right for sounds and upper right for images. Ask the person to update or modify the generalisations and/or beliefs they would now make about the new experience and how different their choices are now.

12. Final step is to ask them to take this new created memory of the event and move it with their eyes to their upper left and now see this is the new remembered memory of the vent. Watch their physiological response. get them to check down to the right for new feelings, down to left for their new internal dialogue and sounds and then back up right to view the new memory again. Let them stay with that as long as they need, even as suggest that they can close their eyes and do this.

SWISH PATTERNS

Swish Patterns involve replacing one Internal Representation or picture with another. A trigger of the present state or current behaviour creates movement and momentum toward a compelling future or new behaviour.

Through Swish Patterns, you install new neurological choices for a new, more compelling behaviour rather than just change or remove old habits (the net effect though is that people's habits will change because they will do a different behaviour instead). This provides the positive **Moving Towards** a desired future goal experience.

The Swish Pattern provides a way to make changes automatic. It is accomplished by having the trigger for the old, un-resourceful state or undesired behaviour cause or trigger new resourceful states and desired behaviours.

This is a useful next step in the event that a persons newly created memory keeps being pushed away by persistent old imagery. You can use the Swish Pattern as a way to dissolve the old imagery and leaving only the mew memory in position.

How To Do A Swish Pattern

1. Rapport/Resourceful states/Outcome.

2. Elicit the present state by asking the client to identify their unwanted behaviour or response.

3. Find the Present State (PS) or behaviour.

Find the **Trigger** in the behaviour or response that the client would like to change. Ask the question, *How do you know when it's time to* _____ *?* This puts the client into the appropriate context where the behaviour occurs. Ask, *When you think of* _____ *, do you have a picture.?*

b) Associate the client into the picture of the present state. *Step into your body and look through your own eyes.* Notice any visible non-verbal cues or shifts as the client associates into the picture.

Direct the client to set that picture aside for now.

4. Create the Desired State (DS) or Desired Behaviour.

   a) Have the client create a picture of themselves if they no longer had their difficulty, the new desired state or behaviour.

b) Change the visual intensity of the desired state using visual submodalities. Note the driver submodalities and use these to make the experience more intense. Build up a really positive, kinaesthetic experience, associated and compelling for the client.

5. Get the client dissociated. Have them step out of the picture.
Use this as a **Break State**.

6. The Set-Up

   a) Bring back the Present State (PS) picture from Steps #3b. Fully associate the client into the picture, looking through their own eyes.

   b) Insert a small, dark picture of the Desired State (DS) from Step #4b in the bottom left corner of the client's vision (assuming the client is Normally Organised. If they are Reverse Organised, insert into the bottom right hand corner). Make sure the client can see their body in the little picture.

7. The Swish

Simultaneously have the Desired State (DS) become bigger and brighter. At the same time, have the Present State (PS) rapidly shrink to nothing in the lower left-hand corner. Accompany this with a "whoosh" or "swish" sound. Please make sure that the sound is not distracting. **Speed is very important**.

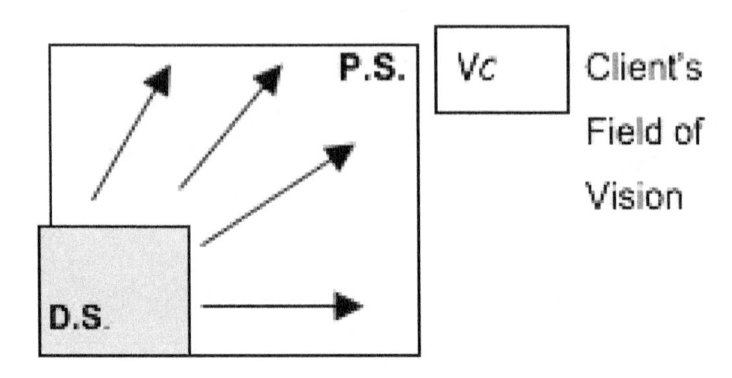

```
                    P.S.   Vc      Client's
         ↗   ↗                     Field of
        /   /  ↘                   Vision
       /   /
      ┌────┐
      │D.S.│  ──→
      └────┘
```

b) Calibrate the client's body shifts. Is there head movement, do their eyes open wider, any muscle tone change, any breathing change?

8. Do the Swish

   a) Clear the screen. Have the client open their eyes (or look away). Always clear the screen after each swish. Often saying 'open your eyes/look away, clear the screen' will suffice. It changes the pattern/breaks the state of the unconscious mind, so that client can move on to step b) below.

   b) Repeat the process at least five times quickly. The client may go slowly at first to become accustomed to technique. Once the client knows the technique each swish should only take a couple of seconds.

9. Test

   a) Ask the client to try to make the Present State picture again.
   b) How have the feelings changed?
   c) This typically becomes more difficult after each Swish.

10. Repeat until the client cannot get the Present State picture back.

11. Test & Future Pace.

KEYS TO SUCCESSFUL SWISH PATTERNS

1. Get the trigger. If the behaviour has already started IT'S
2. TOO LATE!
3. Be fully associated in the old pattern.
4. Have detailed sensory-specific representations in the desired state.
5. Have the client be dissociated in the final state picture - this will result in DIRECTION and MOTIVATION (generally preferred to generate a compelling future). If associated in final state picture, this will result in just the feelings of the OUTCOME, without the desire to change.
6. Make sure to have a break state between each Swish so as not to loop them together. Have the client close their eyes during each step of process and open them between steps. If the client is doing it with their eyes open, get them to look away, or at you.
7. Swish to Visual Construct. For a client with Normally Organised eye patterns, this means that the final state picture will start in the bottom left

hand corner, and explode towards the top right as they look at it ie into their Visual Construct. If the client is Reverse Organised, then start the final state picture in the bottom right hand side and explode towards the top left.

8. Do the Swish quickly. The Unconscious Mind works quickly, so get the client to do it quickly. If they feel you're going too fast, slow down for one go and then accelerate.

"Old picture, new picture, Swish, open your eyes (or look away), clear the screen

Old picture, new picture, Swish, open your eyes (or look away), clear the screen

Old picture, new picture, Swish, open your eyes (or look away), clear the screen

IMPORTANT NOTE:

The Swish Pattern can be used at the end of the Eye Patterning and Re-Imprinting process to erase a stubborn old image that a client is having difficulty removing. Discuss this with your client before using this to ensure that it is ecological for them to do this at that moment. If not revisit another time.

SWISH PATTERN SCRIPT

1. Rapport/Resourceful states/Outcome.
2. "What is the state or behaviour that you would like to change?
3. What do you presently do that you don't want to do?"
4. "How do you know when it's time to _____? When you think of that do you have a picture of what you see just before the unwanted behaviour begins. Step into your body in this picture and look through your own eyes. Set that picture aside for now (PS picture)."
5. "How would you like to feel or act instead? How would you see yourself if you no longer had this behaviour? What would you look like if you were behaving differently? Do you have a picture of you with the behaviour that you want. Make the picture absolutely the right size and brightness for you. Make the colours rich and very compelling for you.
6. Make those feelings just right." (DS picture).

The Immediate Care Process

7. *"Good, now step out of the picture so you see your body in the picture"* (DS). Use this as a Break State.
8. *"Bring back that old picture of the behaviour that you would like to change"*
9. *"What I'd like you to do, not yet but when I tell you to, is to listen for the "*
10. Clear the screen and open your eyes."
11. Break State. Repeat Steps #6 and #7 at least four more times.
12. *"Can you get that picture of that old state or behaviour back?*
13. *Where did the old picture go? Did it change? How about the feelings?*
14. *Did they go away with the picture?"*
15. Repeat until the client cannot get the Present State picture back.
16. Test & Future Pace.

DESIGNER SWISH

The Swish Pattern that has been covered here is the classic Swish Pattern referred to by Richard Bandler in *'Using Your Brain For a Change'*. The drivers are

- size,
- brightness
- associated/dissociated.

For many people, these will be drivers. If however the client's driver's is, say, distance instead of size, then in order to respect the client's model of the world, create a Swish Pattern where distance is used, as opposed to size. So, for example, instead of having the Desired State picture start small and then get big, and the Present State picture start big and get small, make the PS picture disappear into the distance, and the DS picture approach from the distance.

If, say someone is primarily auditory, then construct an auditory Swish Pattern. If a driver is location, ask the client to have the PS sound move to a neutral point, and the DS sound come into the DS location.

Use a similar approach with a kinaesthetic Swish.

FINAL NOTE

I would like to take this final opportunity to thank you for taking part in this experience that I hope has opened your mind to the multitude of possibilities available to you. We are only ever limited by our own imagination and beliefs and when we learn how to change them, we are then so much more capable of exploring life to its fullest potential.

As you are even more aware now, when we learn to change our thoughts and perceptions, we can change our language and our behaviour. Through these changes we ultimately raise the ceiling from our previously held beliefs about our limits and capabilities, and, every time we achieve these changes, we can then raise that bar again, and again, and again.

I truly hope that you take at least one thing of deep value away with you from this and that you continue to make use of that in every aspect of your life where it is applicable.

I wish you all the success and the very best in what ever you do.

Best wishes

Simon Maryan

RECOMMENDED READING

- 101 Trauma Informed Interventions: Activities, Exercises and Assignments to Move the Client and Therapy Forward; Linda A. Curran
- The Biology of Belief: Unleashing the Power of Consciousness, Matter and Miracles; Bruce H Lipton PhD
- Beliefs: Pathways to Health and Wellbeing; Robert Dilts and Tim Halbom
- Flow and the Foundations of Positive Psychology; Mihaly Csikszentmihalyi
- The Structure of Magic, Volumes 1&2: A Book About Language and Therapy; John Grinder and Richard Bandler
- Hypnotic Alteration of Sensory Perceptual and Psychophysical Processes (Collected papers of Milton Erickson)

- My Voice Will Go With You: Teaching Tales of Milton H Erickson
- The Body Keeps the Score: Professor Bessel van der Kolk
- Using Your Brain For A Change: Richard Bandler
- Change Your Mind And Keep The Change: Steve Andreas, Connirae Andreas • An Insider's Guide to Submodalities:
- Richard Bandler and Will MacDonald
- The Psychology of Mind-Body Healing, New Concepts of Therapeutic Hypnosis:
- Ernest Lawrence Rossi
- The Body Remembers, The
- Psychophysiology of Trauma and Trauma
- Treatment: Babette Rothschild
- The Body Remembers Casebook, Unifying
- Methods and Models in the Treatment of
- Trauma and PTSD: Babette Rothschild
- The Body Remembers Vol 2, Revolutionizing Trauma Treatment:
- Babette Rothschild
- Trauma Essentials, The Go-To Guide: Babette Rothschild
- 8 Keys To Safe Trauma Recovery, TakeCharge Strategies To Empower your

- Healing: Babette Rothschild • Waking The Tiger, Healing Trauma: Peter.A.Levine
- The Complex PTSD Workbook, A MindBody Approach to Regaining Emotional
- Control & Becoming Whole: Ariel Schwartz
- PhD
- Limbic System: Hypothalamus, Amygdala, Hippocampus, Septal Nuclei, Cingulate:
- R.Gabriel Josephhat Every Body is Saying:
- Joe Navarro
- The Dictionary of Body Language: Joe Navarro
- The Psychobiology of Mind-Body Healing New Concepts of Therapeutic Hypnosis:
- Ernest L Rossi
- The Biology of Belief: Bruce Lipton PhD
- How Emotions Are Made: Lisa Feldman Barrett
- Molecules of Emotions: Candice.B.Pert PhD
- The Mind - Consciousness, Prediction, and the Brain: E.Bruce Goldstein

Printed in Great Britain
by Amazon